The Art of Eating Well

Simply HEALTHY

DIABETES EDITION

The Art of Eating Well

Simply HEALTHY

DIABETES EDITION

Chef Edwin Cabrera

Sherri Flynt MPH, RD, LDN

Erica Hechler, MS, RD, CDE

Foreword by Damon Tanton, MD

Introduction by Richard Pratley, MD

Photography by Spencer Freeman and Rachel Freeman

Advent
Health
Press

SIMPLY HEALTHY: Diabetes Edition
Copyright © 2019 AdventHealth Press
Published by AdventHealth Press
605 Montgomery Road, Altamonte Springs, Florida 32714

EXTENDING the HEALING MINISTRY of CHRIST

Editor-in-Chief	Todd Chobotar
Managing Editor	Denise Rougeux-Putt
Food Writer	Joseph Hayes
Food Stylist/Food Artist	Anne McLaughlin Nechkov
Diabetes Institute Director	Stephanie Lind, MBA
Project Coordinator	Susan Miner
Promotion	Caryn McCleskey
Production	Lillian Boyd
Copy Editor	Pam Nordberg
Photography	Spencer Freeman
	Rachel Freeman
Creative Development	Timothy Brown
	Kathy Hutson
Database	Matthew Delello
Design	Matt Clark / ImageDesigns.com

PUBLISHER'S NOTE: This book is not intended to replace a one-on-one relationship with a qualified healthcare professional but as a sharing of knowledge and information from the research and experience of the authors. You are advised and encouraged to consult with your healthcare professional in all matters relating to your health and the health of your family. The publisher and authors disclaim any liability arising directly or indirectly from the use of this book.

IMPORTANT NOTES
Weights and Measures: All recipes include customary US and metric measurements. Metric conversions are based on a standard developed for this book and have been rounded off. Actual weights may vary. Time: All times are estimates based on the preparation of original recipes. Actual times may vary.

ACKNOWLEDGEMENTS
Special thanks to Mark Hertling, BS, MS, MA, Jay Perez, MDiv, ACPE,
Don Bartlett, BSRT, RRT, CCA, Frank Carter, James Ammons III, and Katinka Bencs

For volume discounts please contact special sales at:
HealthProducts@FLHosp.org | 407-200-8224

Library of Congress Control number: 2018931081

Designed in the United States of America. Printed in Korea.
PR 17 16 15 14 13 12 11 10 9 8 7 6 5 4 3 2 1
ISBN 13: 978-0-9904191-3-6

For other life changing resources visit:
AdventHealthPress.com
AdventHealthDiabetesInstitute.com
CreationHealth.com

CONTENTS

END NOTES

Foreword

Over the past several decades, the incidence of diabetes and obesity (so-called "diabesity") has risen dramatically. In fact, according to the Centers for Disease Control and Prevention, nearly 1 in 10 Americans now has diabetes. Our genetic predispositions, combined with a gravitation toward sedentary lifestyles and prepackaged, processed foods, has led to the emergence of a verifiable epidemic.

We now live in a marginless world, fraught with escalating stress and incomplete rest . . . a world where quality food has become a luxury and wellness, an afterthought. Unfortunately, we also find ourselves in an era of expanding waistlines and escalating health risks, despite monumental leaps in medical understanding and care.

While I recognize that this all sounds fairly ominous, I also remain confident that we can find a clear pathway that will allow us to break away from the unhealthy lifestyles described above. By developing wise habits, we can often prevent (or at least postpone) diabetes and obesity. This pathway is neither complicated, mysterious, expensive, nor privileged. The process, fortunately, is rather simple—even foundational—and it centers around HARNESSING THE POWER OF NUTRITION. By returning to the nutritional basics and choosing foods that will allow our bodies to heal and our minds to clear, we can take back control. By embracing the fundamental teachings in this cookbook, we can make changes to reassert ownership of our lifestyles. By utilizing the methods laid out by Chef Edwin Cabrera and Nutritionist Sherri Flynt, we can reduce the power of disease and reverse illness. Just think how much more focused we would be if we ate appropriately, and how much more energetic we would feel without excess fat holding us down.

In this cookbook, the authors have included simple, healthy, delectable recipes that result in dishes that are not only a feast for the eyes, but also a pleasure to the palate. The recipes rely heavily on healthy vegetables, fruits, whole grains, beans, fiber, vitamins, minerals, and phytonutrients. Even more importantly, the dishes minimize saturated fats, cholesterol, sugar, and salt, without compromising flavor. A quick perusal of the full-page photos that accompany each dish will convince even the most skeptical that these recipes are creatively designed and surprisingly delicious.

The ancient Chinese proverb says it best: "He who takes medicine and neglects diet wastes the skills of the physician." We must remember that food, at its core, is medicine. Let's not, therefore, devalue or marginalize it. Instead, let's harness its power so we can reclaim a more balanced, healthful life.

Damon Tanton, MD
Medical Director
AdventHealth Diabetes Institute

Tears ran down Hope's face as she sat in my examination room.

I had been caring for Hope since she was diagnosed with type 2 diabetes a couple of years earlier. Like many people, she had resisted the diagnosis. Despite feeling tired and having trouble with her vision, she didn't want to believe diabetes was the problem. "I'm just getting old," she had complained. We had tried several different pills over the last year, but, for whatever reason, these had not brought her symptoms under control. Her hemoglobin A1c was now 13.6%—twice what it should have been.

"Isn't there anything I can do to avoid going on insulin?" she sniffled.

"Well . . . ," I began slowly, "there are several things we can do to get better control of your diabetes. First, I think it would be helpful if you went to our diabetes self-management education classes. I know you read all about diabetes on the Internet, but most people find the classes really useful."

I could see her wrinkling her forehead at the thought of going to a class, but I pushed on. "One thing that our certified diabetes educators focus on is the importance of good nutrition. I also think it would be important to start a regular exercise program. Nothing crazy—just walking for at least 30 minutes a day for starters."

"This would keep me from having to go on insulin?" she asked hopefully.

I shook my head. "Nope. Unfortunately, your blood sugars are so high that diet and exercise alone are unlikely to get your blood sugars to goal."

The loud sniffling returned. "It's just that since I was diagnosed with diabetes, I have been scared about having to go on insulin," she confided. "I've heard so many bad things about diabetes —people going blind or losing their feet. And it seems like these people are always on insulin. I feel like such a failure . . . I have given up."

"You're not a failure," I reassured her. "Many people struggle with these issues. Let me explain. We know that if we can get your blood sugars under control—particularly early on—your risk of serious complications such as vision loss or amputations is very low. Most people with diabetes—even those who have had diabetes for many years—live pretty normal lives."

"We also know," I continued, "that when your blood sugars are very high, insulin secretion and the ability of the body to respond to insulin are impaired; we call this glucotoxicity. The word doesn't matter—what is important is that when your blood sugars are high, your body has an even harder time controlling your blood sugars."

"The good news is that this is reversible. If we can control your blood sugars with insulin for three to four months, your body can recover some of its normal function. We might even be able to go back and try the pills again."

"Well . . . I guess I could try it for a short time if you think it would help," she said reluctantly.

"I know it will help, and I am confident that you can do this!" I said.

Hope returned to my office three months after starting insulin. She seemed brighter and more energetic.

"So . . . how's it going?" I began.

"Great!" she exclaimed. "I have been looking forward to telling you about my progress. First of all, I went to the diabetes class. It really wasn't as bad as I thought it was going to be. I actually learned a lot of things. Plus, I met several people who were having the same sorts of issues I was having. I felt better knowing I wasn't alone.

"The nutrition part of the class was especially good!" she said with gusto. "In fact, I signed up for additional classes and even attended a cooking demonstration with Chef Edwin. I learned that there were several simple things I could do to improve my diet. Now both my husband and I are eating better— although I suspect he sneaks a piece of pie on occasion when I am not looking.

"We have also begun an exercise program," she said. "My husband and I have been walking for 30 minutes after dinner every night."

"That's terrific!" I said. "And how are you doing with the insulin?"

"Well, it wasn't as bad as I had thought it was going to be," she acknowledged. "I was very nervous when your nurse helped me with that first shot, but I hardly even felt it. Now I don't think twice about it. I don't know why I resisted it so long; it's no big deal. And I really feel better! I am less tired and I have more energy during the day."

"How are your blood sugars?" I asked.

"Much better," she said. "Here, look at my record."

It didn't take much time to see that her blood sugars were, in fact, much better. Instead of blood sugars in the 300 to 400 range, most of her blood sugars were now in the 100 to low 200 range. Not perfect, but noticeably improved.

"Looks much better!" I said. "And it goes along with the improvement in hemoglobin A1c I noticed on your labs."

"Oooh . . . what is it?" she asked excitedly.

"8.1%" I said.

"Rats!" she grumbled.

"That's a huge improvement!" I explained.

"I guess so," she said, "but I was hoping it would be normal—or at least under 7%."

"Don't be disappointed. I'm really impressed with your progress," I continued. "You didn't get to a hemoglobin A1c of 13.6% overnight, and you won't be able to normalize it overnight, either. I think the hard work you are putting into diet and exercise is really paying off."

"Maybe you're right," she said. "Actually, I don't feel like the new diet and exercise program is all that hard. I've always been interested in good nutrition and healthy foods. I'm just putting that interest into action now."

"Great!" I said. "Keep at it!"

Hope returned to my office a few months later.

"Guess what? I've lost a total of 40 pounds with the diet and exercise program!" she said proudly.

"That's wonderful. I bet you feel better," I said.

"I do. It seems like my joints don't hurt as much. I was able to join a gym and have been working out almost daily."

"Fantastic. Any problems?" I asked.

"Well . . . I've had to buy a new wardrobe," she chuckled. "But there is one thing I was wondering about. It seems like lots of my blood sugars are in the 80–100 range now. I haven't had any low blood sugar reactions, but I was wondering . . . should I decrease my dose of insulin?"

"Looks like your body is recovering some of its normal function," I said. "Your hemoglobin A1c has improved as well. It's now 6.2%. Let's decrease the dose of insulin and see how you do over the next three months."

Hope did well. Over the next several months her numbers continued to improve and we were eventually able to stop her insulin altogether. When I last saw her in clinic, she had been off insulin for over two years with normal blood sugars and a hemoglobin A1c in the 5.5% range.

THE LESSON OF HOPE

The true story of Hope offers several lessons for all people with diabetes.

- Diabetes is not a death sentence. The great majority of patients with diabetes live happy, productive lives.

- If you control your blood sugars, your chances of having long-term, serious complications are much lower.

- Your body has remarkable healing powers. By controlling your blood sugars, you can improve the efficiency of your body.

- Diet and exercise can be as effective as medicine. Like medicine, they only work when done regularly.

- Insulin is not the treatment of final resort or a last-ditch effort. We often use insulin early after the diagnosis of diabetes to control sugar levels. Sometimes we can stop insulin when the body has recovered enough of its normal function.

- And most of all, never give up hope!

Richard E. Pratley, MD
Samuel E. Crockett Chair in Diabetes Research at AdventHealth Orlando
AdventHealth Diabetes Institute

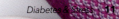

Although you may have heard of diabetes, you may not completely understand what it means. Having a better understanding of what diabetes is and what happens in the body when you have diabetes puts you in a better position to help manage the condition. In the story of Hope (in the foreword), she had fears regarding treatment and what was possible in terms of management that were addressed the more she learned about what diabetes is. For some of you, this may be a refresher, but for many others, this may be an important first step in understanding this condition. The more we understand what something is, the better position we are in to successfully take it on.

WHAT IS DIABETES?

Diabetes is a disease that causes high glucose in the blood because the body is not able to make enough insulin or is not able to use the insulin properly. Too much blood glucose—also called blood sugar—leads to serious health issues.

WHAT IS THE PANCREAS?

The pancreas is a small organ located in the left side of your abdomen. The pancreas helps your body digest food as well as make insulin. Insulin helps turn the sugar from carbohydrates into energy and allows the body to store glucose in its cells for future use.

THREE TYPES OF DIABETES

- **Type 1 diabetes:** With type 1 diabetes, the pancreas makes little or no insulin. People with type 1 diabetes must take insulin every day.

- **Type 2 diabetes:** With type 2 diabetes, the pancreas does not make enough insulin or the cells are unable to use insulin well. People with type 2 diabetes often need to take pills, insulin, or other injected medicines. Type 2 is the most common type of diabetes.

- **Gestational diabetes:** With gestational diabetes, the cells do not use insulin well in the middle or late stages of pregnancy. When the baby is delivered, this type of diabetes usually goes away in 90–95 percent of women. Unless some lifestyle changes are made, however, up to 60 percent of these women will develop type 2 diabetes within 10 to 20 years.

COMPLICATIONS OF DIABETES

To understand diabetes and all that it entails, we must realize that some serious complications can arise in those who have the disease. We mention this here not to cause panic or scare you, but because awareness of the problems that can arise in connection with diabetes is crucial. Once you know the various health complications associated with diabetes, you have a better chance of approaching the condition with the consideration and care it deserves, and you will be more aware of the signs and symptoms as they present themselves.

Remember that in the story of Hope, she had a lot of fears regarding the complications of diabetes. Those fears were keeping her from properly addressing and managing the situation. Running in the other direction, however, does not address the risks involved. But when you make the choice to get healthy and get diabetes under control, you will be doing a lot to help reduce your risks of all the complications associated with diabetes. And that's a great thing!

Diabetes complications and related conditions include the following:

- **Heart disease and stroke:** People with diabetes are twice as likely to have heart disease or a stroke as people without diabetes—and at an earlier age.

- **Blindness and other eye problems:** Diabetic retinopathy (damage to blood vessels in the retina), cataracts (clouding of the lens), and glaucoma (increase in fluid pressure in the eye) can all result in vision loss.

- **Kidney disease:** High blood sugar levels can damage the kidneys long before a person has symptoms. Kidney damage can cause chronic kidney disease, which can lead to kidney failure.

- **Amputations:** Diabetes damages blood vessels and nerves, particularly in the feet, and can lead to serious, hard-to-treat infections. Amputation is sometimes necessary to stop the spread of infection. [1]

WHAT ABOUT MEDICATIONS?

Just as Hope had fears regarding taking medications for her diabetes, you may be afraid as well. This is a normal reaction for most people who are new to diabetes. They wonder if taking medications may make things worse, or perhaps it makes the fact of having diabetes all too real for them. Whatever the reason for your fears, speaking openly and honestly with your doctor regarding any hesitations you may have about taking diabetes medications is important. Your doctor can guide you to the best route possible to be able to reduce or stop taking diabetes medications if at all possible.

When dealing with diabetes, make sure to meet with your doctor to learn how your medications may interact with the foods you eat.

Eating Healthy

Most of us eat three meals per day, but we give little thought to the impact that food has on our overall health. Sure, we know that eating healthy can make a difference, but we don't give much thought to exactly how big a difference it can make. In the story of Hope, she was reluctant at first to attend classes to learn about healthy eating, but once she did, they had a huge impact on her life. Not only did she lose significant weight, but she felt better, had more energy, and gained a valuable understanding of the importance of eating healthier. She even used that information to get her husband to eat healthier.

Take your time to think about and enjoy your positive food choices. This book is here to help! Food has a major role in managing diabetes because it raises blood glucose. The body turns food into glucose. What you eat and how much food you eat affects your blood glucose. In many people, losing weight can improve or even reverse diabetes.

BASIC GUIDELINES FOR EATING

You may have been eating every day for your whole life, but people don't often think about the best way to go about eating. Guidelines for eating each day are especially important for those with diabetes. If you follow these guidelines, you will be in a better position to help your body be healthier and improve or reverse your diabetes.

Eat at least three meals every day. Do not skip meals—especially breakfast.

- This helps you spread your calories throughout the day and control the amount of glucose going into your blood during the day. It also helps prevent you from becoming too hungry, which can lead to overeating at meals.

Space your meals four to five hours apart.

- This also helps to control hunger and overeating. Most important, this helps prevent low blood glucose—if you take diabetes medicine—by keeping a balance between glucose from food and medicine in the blood.

Eat a snack that contains carbohydrates when meals are more than six hours apart.

- Sometimes meals become delayed by more than an hour due to your home or work schedule. A snack can help steady your blood glucose and keep it from dropping too low. Use snacks as part of your meal plan. Limit yourself to one to two servings of carbohydrates per snack, and be sure to include a serving of protein and/or fat as well.

Avoid fasting for more than 12 hours.

- Fasting means not eating or drinking any calories in over eight hours. Skipping meals and snacks causes low blood sugar levels.

Balance your meal plate with carbohydrates, proteins, and fats.

- Spreading out the carbohydrates you eat during the day helps balance your meal plate. A variety of whole foods also helps to add more vitamins, minerals, and fiber to your meals.

Control your food portion sizes at each meal.

- Eating about the same amount of carbohydrates every day is important. This helps keep blood glucose levels stable.

Drink plenty of water

- Staying hydrated is essential, and water is the best beverage choice of all. Aim for six to eight 8-ounce glasses per day. If you get tired of plain water, try adding a squeeze of lemon or lime, or your favorite ingestible essential oil for variety. Try sparkling water, infused water, or unsweetened regular or herbal tea.

- Avoid sweetened beverages like sweetened fruit juices and fruit drinks, soda, sweet tea, sports drinks, energy drinks, and other sweetened drinks. These add empty calories and carbohydrates without adding nutrition. [2]

MAJOR NUTRIENTS OF A MEAL

In the story of Hope, she learned at the classes she attended how important nutrition is. She even took it a step further and went to a cooking demonstration and signed up for additional classes. Nutrition is an important issue, especially when it comes to diabetes. When you understand more about the nutrition aspects of your meal, you can strive to make better, healthier choices.

Eating well-balanced meals helps control your diabetes. This means eating a wide variety of healthy foods, limiting portion sizes, following a meal plan low in saturated fat, and controlling your intake of carbohydrates. This will help control your glucose. A healthy meal plan includes food choices from the three major types of foods—carbohydrate, protein, and fat.

CARBOHYDRATES

Starch, fiber, and sugar are carbohydrates. Carbohydrates turn into sugar faster and in greater quantity than protein or fats. They are ideal for quickly treating low blood glucose. See food lists in the next section for portion sizes. Many carbohydrates are good sources of vitamins, minerals, and may also contain fiber.

TYPES OF CARBOHYDRATES

- Starches such as grains, breads, starchy vegetables

- Sugars such as fruits, milk, yogurt, added sugar, and sweets

- Fiber, found in food from plants such as vegetables, fruits, grains, beans, and lentils

Research suggests that there is no one ideal amount of carbohydrate that a person should eat. Carbohydrate amounts are counted in grams. Limiting the portion size of carbohydrates can help maintain blood glucose levels and control calories.

ADDED SUGAR

The American Diabetes Association recommends eating patterns that reduce the intake of foods containing added sugars. It advises the intake of carbohydrates from vegetables, fruits, whole grains, beans, peas, and dairy products in place of carbohydrate sources containing added sugars, fats, or sodium. These healthier, "nutrient-dense" carbohydrates are great sources of dietary fiber, vitamins, minerals, and other beneficial substances that have positive health effects. [3]

FIBER

The minimum daily amount of fiber an average person should consume is 25 grams for women and 38 grams for men. Most Americans get 15 grams or less. You can increase your fiber intake by eating more whole grains, beans, fruit, vegetables, and nuts. The American Diabetes Association follows the FDA recommendations that at least half of the grains you eat should be whole grains (for example, oatmeal, brown rice, whole-grain pasta, or whole wheat bread) and that you should limit your intake of refined grains and products made with refined grains (for example, Cream of Wheat, white rice, white pasta, or white bread [4]). Fiber can help reduce the amount of fat and cholesterol your body absorbs, which can help lower your LDL ("bad") cholesterol [5]. Fiber may also slow the rate at which carbohydrates are released into the bloodstream, which could help prevent rapid rises in your blood glucose after a meal.

CARBOHYDRATE FOODS

One serving is about 15 grams of carbohydrate
Starches: Grains and Starchy Vegetables

Grains
- 1 slice bread (1 ounce)
- 1 tortilla (6-inch size)
- ¼ large bagel (1 ounce)
- 2 taco shells (5-inch size)
- ½ hamburger or hot dog bun
- ¾ cup ready-to-eat unsweetened cereal
- ½ cup cooked cereal
- 4 to 6 small crackers
- 1/3 cup pasta or rice (cooked)
- ¾–1 ounce pretzels or tortilla chips

Starchy Vegetables
- 3 cups popcorn (popped)
- ½ cup beans, peas, lentils, corn, sweet potatoes, or mashed or boiled potatoes (cooked)
- 1 cup winter squash
- ¼ large baked potato (3 ounces)
- Butternut squash, acorn squash—½–¾ cup
- Yam—½ cup
- Plantain—1/3 cup

Fruits

1 small fresh fruit (about 4 ounces), ¾ to 1 cup chopped fresh fruit or ½ cup canned or frozen fruit

2 tablespoons dried fruit (blueberries, cherries, cranberries, mixed fruit, raisins)

- 1 small apple
- 4 apricots
- ½ banana
- Blackberries
- Blueberries
- Cantaloupe
- Cherries
- ½ grapefruit
- Grapes
- Honeydew melon
- Kiwi
- Mango
- Nectarine
- Orange
- Papaya
- Peaches
- Pears
- Pineapple
- Plums
- Raspberries
- Strawberries
- Tangerines
- Watermelon

Dairy

- 1 cup fat-free or low-fat milk
- 1 cup soy milk
- ⅔ cup (6 ounces) nonfat yogurt sweetened with sugar-free sweetener

Non-starchy vegetables are also considered carbohydrates, but they contain very small amounts. They are also generally low in calories. There is no limit on the amounts that you can include with your meals or snacks.

Non-Starchy Vegetables

- Artichoke hearts
- Asparagus
- Bamboo shoots

- Green beans
- Bean sprouts
- Beets
- Brussels sprouts
- Broccoli
- Cabbage
- Bok choy
- Carrots
- Cauliflower
- Celery
- Cucumber
- Daikon
- Eggplant
- Collard greens
- Kale
- Hearts of palm
- Mushrooms
- Okra
- Onions
- Pea pods
- Peppers
- Radishes
- Sauerkraut
- Spinach
- Squash
- Sugar snap peas
- Tomato
- Turnips
- Water chestnuts

PROTEIN

The body needs protein for growth, healing, and building muscle. Include a protein source in your meals and snacks to help you feel fuller and to replace some of the carbohydrates. Protein comes from either an animal or plant source.

Current research states that, by itself, protein appears to have little effect on blood glucose when eaten in amounts of three to four ounces—about the size of the palm of your hand. Protein in a meal can cause a slower increase in blood glucose.

Plant-based protein foods such as beans, lentils, hummus, black-eyed peas, and edamame are high in fiber and healthy fats, and provide a good quality of protein without increasing the amount of cholesterol in your diet. Limit your intake of red meat such as beef, which is often high in saturated fat and cholesterol, and processed meat like hot dogs, deli meats, and bacon, which are high in saturated fat and sodium.[6]

Protein Foods
- Meats: beef, chicken, fish, seafood, turkey, lamb
- Meat substitutes: cheese, egg, egg substitute, tofu, beans, peas, nuts, nut butters, soy, processed meat alternatives, and hummus

*Note: some meat substitutes may contain carbohydrates, which need to be counted in your meal plan

FAT

Your body uses fat to provide fat-soluble vitamins—A, D, E, and K—to make hormones and to maintain healthy cells. Fat adds flavor and helps keep you full. It takes longer than carbohydrates and protein to break down and be absorbed by the body. Fat does not break down into glucose, and it does not cause blood glucose to rise. A high-fat meal causes your stomach to empty slower, which can keep glucose levels high for a longer period of time after you eat.

The type of fat you eat is important. Fats can be categorized as either "healthy" fats or "unhealthy" fats.[7]

Healthy fats include monounsaturated and polyunsaturated fats, and omega-3 fatty acids. Sources include:

- **Monounsaturated fat:** Olives, avocados, peanuts and peanut butter, almonds, cashews, and pecans.

- **Polyunsaturated fat:** Vegetable oils such as safflower and sunflower oils, pumpkin and sunflower seeds, walnuts, and salad dressings.

- **Omega-3 fatty acids:** Fish such as salmon, albacore tuna, and sardines; plant sources include flaxseed and flaxseed oil, tofu, and walnuts.

Unhealthy fats include saturated fat, trans fats, and cholesterol. These can increase your risk of heart disease, stroke, and type 2 diabetes.

- Saturated fat is found mostly in foods of animal origin, including beef, lamb, pork, chicken skins, lard, butter, and cheese.

- Trans fat tends to be hidden in food. Look for "partially hydrogenated vegetable oil" on the label. You will find trans fat in pastries such as cakes, pies, doughnuts, and cookies, as well as in stick margarine, crackers, microwave popcorn, frozen pizza, and fried fast foods.

- Cholesterol is a necessary component needed by your body to build cells. Your body produces all the cholesterol it needs, so you don't need to include cholesterol in your diet. Having too much cholesterol in the blood is associated with heart disease and other cardiovascular problems. Cholesterol is found in animal products, including meat, poultry, and full-fat dairy products.

Fats are high in calories—one tablespoon gives a whopping 120 calories—so limiting even the healthy fats is a good idea, especially for weight reduction. Where possible, choose cold-pressed, extra-virgin oils. They contain more vitamin E and beneficial phytochemicals than regular vegetable oils.

Fat Foods

- Olives
- Oils
- Nuts: walnuts, almonds, cashews, pistachios, pecans, peanuts
- Nut butters
- Avocado
- Seeds: pumpkin, sunflower, sesame
- Salad dressing
- Margarine
- Butter
- Mayonnaise

DIABETES SUPERFOODS

Some foods are so packed with healthy vitamins, minerals, antioxidants, and fiber that they deserve a "diabetes superfood" label. These include beans and peas, dark green leafy vegetables, sweet potatoes, berries, citrus fruits, nuts, whole grains, high omega-3 fish (like salmon), and low-fat and low-sugar yogurt. Try to include as many of these in your daily food plan as possible.[8]

CREATING A HEALTHY MEAL PLAN

Creating a healthy meal plan will provide you with guidelines and help to manage your blood glucose. Think of your meal patterns as a lifestyle, not a short-term diet.

THE HEALTHY PLATE METHOD

The "Healthy Plate" method is used to guide people on what type of food—carbohydrate, protein and fat—to include at meal times. It is an easy way to begin meal planning. It helps you create a balanced meal by choosing a variety of foods, allowing for foods to be eaten in the right amounts without having to measure.

Using a nine-inch plate, practice the following system: Fill half of the plate with non-starchy vegetables and the other half with one serving of healthy protein (one-quarter of the plate) and one serving of healthy carbohydrates (the other quarter of the plate).

Estimate Your Food Portions by This Easy Rule of Thumb

PALM = ABOUT 3 OUNCES   FIST = ABOUT 1 CUP   THUMB = 1 TABLESPOON OR 1 OUNCE

TIPS FOR EATING OUT

Don't assume that having diabetes means you can't eat out. You absolutely can, but knowing how to make some healthier choices is going to help you manage your diabetes better. Keep these tips in mind when dining out:

- Use the Healthy Plate method to fill your food plate
- Share a meal, or plan to use a take-out container if portions are too large
- Ask for foods to be prepared without extra butter or added sugars
- Ask for salad dressings, sauces, gravies, and condiments to be provided on the side
- Limit foods that are breaded or fried
- Beware of the offers that include the words "jumbo," "giant," "biggie-sized," "super-sized," or "all you can eat"
- Choose entrees that are small or of moderate size—a taco instead of a large burrito, or a regular hamburger versus a large burger with three slices of bread
- Choose chicken sandwiches that are grilled instead of fried
- Try to dine out less if possible

NUTRITIONAL LABEL TIPS

You have seen nutrition labels many times, but you may not stop to look at them. Now is a great time to become an avid label reader. It's the best way to see what is really in the food you are buying and determine if it is something you should limit or even avoid, or if it's a food you should embrace with gusto.

The Nutrition Facts panel on a food label shows the total carbohydrates for one serving in grams. Use these tips to help you choose the portion size:

1. Look at the label's serving size.
2. Check the grams of total carbohydrates. This is the amount of carbohydrates in one serving.
3. Divide the grams of total carbohydrates by 15. This number equals the number of carbohydrate servings in one serving. Remember: One carbohydrate serving is 15 grams.

NOTE: The grams of sugar are already included in the total carbohydrate amount, so you don't need to count those separately.

MEAL PREPARATION TIPS

Involve the whole family, and make a weekly plan for meals and staying on track. Planning meals and cooking together can be a great opportunity to share in the joy of healthy eating. Shop smart, make a list, and stick to it. Choose frozen or pre-cut vegetables to save time. Limit processed food and read the nutritional labels before you buy.

Perhaps the last thing you want to hear is that it is important to become more active. Many people cringe at hearing this, but, once they begin to do it, they feel the difference it makes in their life. In the story of Hope, she found that even taking short walks each day was beneficial. People often say they don't have time to exercise, but the amazing benefits make it something that should be on everyone's priority list.

There are several benefits to exercise and managing your diabetes. Your body uses insulin better and thus helps to control your blood glucose when you exercise. Being active improves your mood, reduces stress, and leads to better nighttime sleep. With all these benefits, let's look at some tips to get you moving.

SETTING A GOAL

Even a little increased activity will help manage your blood glucose. Talk to your doctor about any limits you may have to exercising before you begin. Set a goal of 30 minutes of intense activity three or four times a week. A few simple ways to increase your activity are to park farther away, use the stairs, walk to someone's desk rather than call on the phone, walk at lunch, or walk your dog after dinner.

GETTING STARTED

Start slowly and with simple movements. Repeat every 10 minutes or so. Simple activity can improve your mood, lower your blood pressure, make your heart stronger, and help you feel more energized. Slowly work up to 30 minutes of activity a day over a week to ten days.

EXERCISE TIPS

Taking small steps can make a big difference. Wear your diabetes alert bracelet. Have a snack and fast-acting sugar with you in case your blood glucose is low. Check your blood glucose if you have symptoms of high or low blood glucose. Also, check your blood glucose before and after your exercise.

- Protect your feet by wearing well-fitting socks and shoes
- Make sure your activity is safe
- Warm up before exercising, and cool down after
- When weather is bad, you can do an indoor activity
- Choose an exercise or activity that you enjoy and is easy for you
- Join a walking group or a club that does activities you like
- Dance to your favorite music
- Involve your family and friends
- Remember to drink plenty of water

Commit to adding exercise to your life each week and see what a difference it can make in your body, mind, and spirit—including your diabetes.

If you feel like you are often stressed out, you're not alone. We live in a fast-paced world today that has people strapped for time and doing far more than they should. The stress of daily life adds up and can take a serious toll on your health. Getting stress under control is a good step in the right direction in helping to care for your diabetes, as well as your overall health and quality of life.

We all have stress in our life, such as being stuck in traffic, having lots of work at our jobs or school, worrying about loved ones, or caring for a sick family member. Managing stress is important to help manage your blood glucose. Stress can cause your blood glucose levels to go too high or too low.

MANAGING STRESS

- **Exercise Regularly.** Physical exercise can release both physical and emotional tension. The key is to find a form of exercise you enjoy and do it regularly.

- **Get Plenty of Sleep.** Sleep plays an important role in your physical health. For example, sleep is involved in healing and repair of your heart and blood vessels. Low amounts of sleep make it harder for your body to get healthy and stay healthy.

- **Use Relaxation Techniques.** Relax the body and mind. Try yoga, meditation, tai chi, biofeedback, deep breathing, progressive muscle relaxation, listening to music, being out in nature, journaling, and other hobbies. Again, the key is to find one or more that you enjoy and can do regularly.

- **Avoid Using Alcohol, Tobacco, or Drugs.** Alcohol, over-the-counter medications, illicit drugs, and tobacco affect your health and well-being. If you smoke, talk to your healthcare provider about ways to quit.

- **Create a Strong Support Network.** Family, friends, or support groups can help. Express your feelings and talk things over with someone you trust. Look for diabetes resources in the community or find support in faith-based groups.

- **Consider Prayer.** Praying can be a way of releasing your worries, frustrations, and fears by entrusting them to God. Prayer can also help you take a few steps back from your current situation and help you to look at your problems in a new and fresh way.

- **Practice Forgiveness.** Not only are anger and stress related, but they can have a very negative impact on your health. Anger has even been linked to hypertension and heart disease. Learn to forgive others for both the intentional and unintentional ways they have hurt you. Practicing forgiveness releases anger and stress, which can lead to better health.

Good Food for Every Body: About These Recipes

The delightful recipes in this cookbook have been created with your whole family in mind. While the recipes do adhere to certain guidelines that make them well-suited for individuals with diabetes, we believe everyone in the family will enjoy these delicious, nutritious dishes. This is great news for the family chef, who will not need to prepare a separate menu for the diabetic family member, saving valuable time and simplifying meal preparation. The nutritional analysis for each of the recipes is a convenient feature that allows you to see the per-serving number of calories, fat, carbohydrates, and more.

CATEGORY TAGS

Along with the nutritional analysis for each recipe, you will also find a list of category tags. The category tags make it easier to identify recipes that meet individual preferences and needs. Many people want to avoid or reduce certain foods in their diet. Others would like to increase certain foods in their eating patterns. Category tags make this process easier. Trying to eat fewer carbs? Lower your intake of sodium? Choose vegan recipes? A quick look at the category tags for each recipe will tell you instantly if it's a recipe you want to use. The sections below explain each of the tags.

CATEGORY TAGS:

- ◉ gluten-free
- ◉ high fiber
- ○ high protein
- ○ low calorie
- ◉ low carbohydrate / low sugar
- ◉ low cholesterol
- ○ low fat / low saturated fat
- ◉ low sodium
- ◉ vegan
- ◉ vegetarian
- ◉ whole food plant based
- ○ whole grain

NUTRITIONAL DATA:

calories	148
fat	12g
sat fat	0.65g
cholesterol	0mg
sodium	125mg
carbohydrates	7g
fiber	3g
sugars	1.78g
protein	6g

LOWER CARB/LOWER SUGAR

This tag means the recipe contains 30 grams or less of total carbohydrates per serving, including added sugars. The American Heart Association recommends limiting added sugars to no more than half of your daily "nonessential" calorie allowance. A simple rule of thumb for most people is the following:

Women: no more than 100 calories of added sugar, which is 6 teaspoons or 24 grams of sugar per day.
Men: no more than 150 calories of added sugar, which is 9 teaspoons or 36 grams of sugar per day.

These amounts include the sugar included in packaged food, not just the sugar you add to your food or drinks. Learn to read labels. Remember that there are four calories in one gram of sugar. So, if a food contains 20 grams of sugar per serving, that adds 80 calories just from the sugar in the product, not including the other ingredients.[9]

Individual carbohydrate requirements vary per person. Be sure to speak to your registered dietitian about what your specific needs are.

LOW FAT/LOW SATURATED FAT

This tag means the recipe contains 3 grams or less of fat per serving. A good rule of thumb is to aim for no more than 3 grams of fat per 100 calories in a dish.

LOW SODIUM

This tag means the recipe contains 140 milligrams or less of sodium per serving. The American Diabetes Association recommends that people with diabetes aim to have 2,300 mg or less of sodium per day. Based on other medical conditions or age, your healthcare provider may recommend even less. Be sure to speak to your medical doctor about what your specific needs are.

VEGAN

This tag means the recipe does not contain any ingredients of animal origin—no beef, pork, poultry, fish, eggs, cheese, milk or other dairy products, honey, or gelatin.

VEGETARIAN (LACTO-OVO)

This tag means the recipe does not contain any animal meat. This recipe may contain ingredients with dairy products such as milk, eggs, and cheese. The prefix "lacto" refers to milk, and the prefix "ovo" refers to eggs.

WHOLE GRAIN

This tag means the recipe contains grains that are considered "intact." A whole grain consists of three parts or layers—the bran, the endosperm, and the germ. The bran is the outer layer of the grain that provides dietary fiber, B vitamins, trace minerals, and antioxidants. The endosperm (the inner part) contains the carbohydrate and protein. The germ contains B vitamins, vitamin E, trace minerals, antioxidants, and essential fats.

GLUTEN-FREE

This tag means the recipe does not contain gluten, a protein found in wheat and other grains such as barley and rye. When selecting ingredients for these recipes (such as oats, quinoa, soy sauce, Worcestershire sauce), ensure that they are labeled "gluten-free" if you intend for the dish to be entirely free of gluten.

WHOLE-FOOD, PLANT-BASED

This tag means the recipe and its ingredients are centered on fruits, vegetables, whole grains, legumes, and/or tubers. A recipe with this tag excludes animal products such as meat, dairy, and eggs, and foods considered to be highly processed or refined such as white flour and refined sugars.

HIGH FIBER

This tag means the recipe contains 3 or more grams of fiber per serving. The American Heart Association recommends 25 grams of fiber for women and 38 grams of fiber for men per day.

LOW CALORIE

This tag means the recipe contains 40 calories or less per serving.

LOW CHOLESTEROL

This tag means the recipe restricts ingredients that contain animal fat, including meats, egg yolk, cream, butter, and milk, all of which contain cholesterol.

For over 100 years, AdventHealth has been encouraging everyone to live life to the fullest—to embrace a lifestyle that promotes health in all aspects of life: mentally, physically, spiritually, and socially. This philosophy of whole-person health is expressed by eight universal principles that form the acronym CREATION. The CREATION Health lifestyle has a long, proven history of wellness and longevity worldwide. We encourage you to adopt these principles to live a healthier, happier life!

Here is a brief overview of the CREATION acronym and its eight principles:

 CHOICE

You have an incredible power in you: the power to choose. Choice is the first step toward vibrant health because those who believe they are in control of their lives tend to live longer and healthier than those who feel they have no control. Choose to live the healthiest life possible by making good lifestyle choices each and every day. Choose health. Choose life!

R REST

In our fast-paced society, we often try to squeeze so much into each day that we neglect to recharge our batteries sufficiently by restorative sleep. Aim to get 7–8 hours every night. But the R in Rest doesn't only refer to getting good sleep; it also means taking time each day to relax. Rest rejuvenates the mind, body, and spirit, empowering you to function at your best. It can even lower your blood pressure and reduce stress! Take some time each day to do something relaxing: go for a stroll in nature, listen to peaceful music, read something inspiring, or play a musical instrument. In addition, take one day a week and make it a day of rest—a day where you avoid the normal work you do during the week and spend time building relationships. Spend time in nature, attend a house of worship, volunteer to serve someone in need. Every area of your life will be enhanced when you give your body, mind, and spirit the rest it needs.

ENVIRONMENT

We interact with the world around us through our five senses. What you see, hear, taste, smell, and feel influences your overall health. Engage your five senses with nature and the natural world in every way you can. Fresh air, sunshine, and the sights, smells, and sounds of nature energize us and give us a sense of peace and well-being. In your home or workspace, bring nature in as much as possible. A plant, a picture of nature, nature sounds, diffusing essential oils, or playing relaxing music can create an atmosphere of peace and tranquility. Think of a peaceful garden and try to make the spaces you spend time in look and feel more like nature.

A ACTIVITY

Physical activity strengthens the body, sharpens the mind, and invigorates the spirit. Engaging in regular physical and mental exercise can greatly improve your quality of life. Be intentional about incorporating more activity into your day. Look for ways to move more, walk more, and stretch more. Even moderate walking is beneficial. Start there and work your way up to more challenging forms of exercise. For mental activity, try doing things like puzzles, word searches, and other games that will stimulate your mind and keep it active. Working on creative hobbies can also engage your mind and keep it active. Find a creative outlet you enjoy such as painting, sculpting, writing, drawing, or craft-making.

TRUST IN GOD

Trust promotes healing and security in your relationship with family, friends, and coworkers, as well as with God or a higher power. Nurturing trust in all your relationships creates inner stability and confidence, which leads to wellness. Talk to your trusted friends, family members, or pastor about your spiritual and emotional needs. Take a few quiet moments each day to meditate, pray, read scripture, or journal about your spiritual thoughts and experiences.

 ## INTERPERSONAL RELATIONSHIPS

We were made for relationships, and healthy interpersonal relationships can produce healing and wholeness in our lives. Social connection fortifies resolve and nourishes the mind, body, and spirit. Think beyond yourself to those around you. Become a good listener. Encourage family and friends to visit you—and drop in to visit them when appropriate. Stay connected with important people in your life through emails, blogs, letters, and phone calls. Keep in mind that not all relationships are healthy. Some toxic relationships can have a negative impact on your health. When it comes to relationships, keep the best, release the rest.

 ## OUTLOOK

Outlook creates your reality. Your mind can have a powerful effect on your body. A positive attitude can strengthen the health of your mind, body, and spirit. Begin a gratitude journal and write down three things you are thankful for each day. When you wake up in the morning, be grateful for another day of life. Keep a list of how you are integrating CREATION Health principles into your life. Choose to look for the positives in situations.

NUTRITION

Nutrition is the fuel that drives you. Vegetables, fruits, beans, whole grains, nuts, and seeds are powerhouses of nutrition and provide maximum benefit for your body. Minimize your intake of processed foods and increase your consumption of unprocessed, natural foods to feel better and more energized. Small changes to your diet can produce profound improvements to your overall health!

TRANSFORM YOUR LIFE THROUGH CREATION HEALTH

Embracing the CREATION Health prescription can help restore health, happiness, balance, and joy to life. People just like you are making a few simple changes in their lives and living longer, fuller lives. They are getting healthy, staying healthy, and are able to do the things they love, well into their later years. Now is the time to join them by transforming your habits into a healthy lifestyle.

If you would like to learn more about CREATION Health, please check out the many resources available at **www.CREATIONHealth.com**.

BREAKFAST

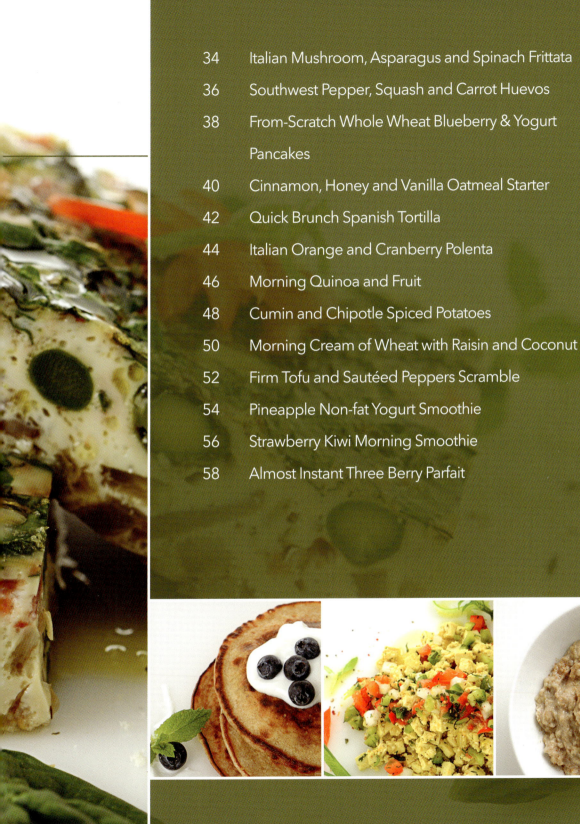

Italian Mushroom, Asparagus and Spinach Frittata

An Italian frittata is neither scrambled eggs nor omelet, so resist the urge to take a fork to stir the cooking eggs or raise the heat. Low in fat and high in iron and minerals, this frittata gets its health benefits from egg whites and fresh vegetables. The frittata enjoys a slow cook with all ingredients firming up at the same time. Pan cooking gives the bottom a chance to brown, while its time in the oven creates a firm yet custardy interior. Save some slices for a cold lunch.

PREP INSTRUCTIONS:

Yield: 4 servings
Prep Time: 7 minutes

Cooking Time: 12 minutes
Total Time: 20 minutes

RECIPE INGREDIENTS:

5 large eggs
1/16 teaspoon kosher salt
¼ teaspoon ground black pepper
¼ cup mushrooms, sliced
¼ cup yellow onions, chopped
½ teaspoon fresh garlic, minced

½ teaspoon Italian Seasoning
¼ cup asparagus, cut into 1" lengths and steamed
½ cup plum tomatoes, diced
¼ cup spinach, shredded
½ tablespoon fresh basil, chopped
nonstick cooking spray

INSTRUCTIONS:

Preheat oven to 350 °F.

Follow prep technique next to each ingredient.

Mix the eggs with the salt and pepper in a small bowl.

In an oven-safe skillet coated with nonstick cooking spray sauté the mushrooms, adding water to avoid sticking. Follow with the onions, garlic, tomatoes, Italian seasoning and the steamed asparagus. Add the basil and half the egg mixture. Then add spinach and the rest of the egg mixture. As soon as the mixture starts to set, place the skillet in the oven and bake for seven minutes or until eggs are firm.

CATEGORY TAGS:

- ◉ gluten-free
- ○ high fiber
- ○ high protein
- ○ low calorie
- ◉ low carbohydrate / low sugar
- ○ low cholesterol
- ○ low fat / low saturated fat
- ○ low sodium
- ○ vegan
- ◉ vegetarian
- ○ whole food plant based
- ○ whole grain

NUTRITIONAL DATA:

calories	105.30
fat	5.99g
sat fat	1.97g
cholesterol	232.50mg
sodium	172.35mg
carbohydrates	3.69g
fiber	0.71g
sugars	1.90g
protein	8.66g

Southwest Pepper, Squash and Carrot Huevos

Give breakfast a Southwestern flair with this easy omelet. Chipotle and chili pepper provide a warm spiciness, while cumin and zucchini is a natural taste union. This omelet is so chock-full of vegetables it will make a perfect start to the day or a healthy low-fat, high-fiber lunch item, and it is hearty enough to save and serve as a cold side dish. For quick individual servings, try pouring the egg mixture into a cooking spray-prepared muffin tin and bake for 5 minutes until set.

PREP INSTRUCTIONS:

Yield: 4 servings

Prep Time: 5 minutes

Cooking Time: 10 minutes

Total Time: 15 minutes

RECIPE INGREDIENTS:

½ cup yellow onion, diced

¼ teaspoon ground cumin

½ teaspoon chili powder

½ cup carrot, shredded

½ cup red bell pepper, diced

½ cup zucchini squash, diced

¼ teaspoon ground chipotle

½ tomato, diced

5 large eggs

¼ teaspoon kosher salt

1 tablespoon cilantro, chopped

nonstick cooking spray

INSTRUCTIONS:

Preheat oven to 350 ° F.

Follow the prep technique next to each ingredient.

In a small skillet sauté the onions, peppers, zucchini, carrots and spices with nonstick cooking spray, except the tomatoes. When vegetables start to caramelize, (adding water if necessary) beat the eggs with the salt and cilantro. Fold into the sautéed vegetables. Place the tomatoes on top and cook on the stove until the bottom of the eggs start to set. Transfer the pan to the oven and bake for 8-10 minutes or until golden on top.

CATEGORY TAGS:

- ◉ gluten-free
- ○ high fiber
- ○ high protein
- ○ low calorie
- ◉ low carbohydrate / low sugar
- ○ low cholesterol
- ○ low fat / low saturated fat
- ○ low sodium
- ○ vegan
- ◉ vegetarian
- ○ whole food plant based
- ○ whole grain

NUTRITIONAL DATA:

calories	117.08
fat	6.11g
sat fat	1.98g
cholesterol	232.50mg
sodium	278.05mg
carbohydrates	6.19g
fiber	1.38g
sugars	3.55g
protein	8.87g

From-Scratch Whole Wheat Blueberry & Yogurt Pancakes

Far better than a packaged pancake mix, and easier than going out for breakfast (and better for your health). It's recipes like this that remind you of the days when most food was made from scratch, and actually had taste and reliably good ingredients. Whole grain flour and yogurt provide fiber, calcium and a good source of probiotics. Give the pancake batter a minute or two to activate in liquid before starting the griddle process; it makes for a lighter pancake with more air bubbles.

PREP INSTRUCTIONS:

Yield: 5 (1/2 cup) servings
Serving Size: 2 pancakes
Prep Time: 6 minutes

Cooking Time: 8 minutes
Total Time: 15 minutes

RECIPE INGREDIENTS:

1 whole egg
1 cup 1% milk
½ tablespoon canola oil
½ teaspoon vanilla extract
2 tablespoons Greek yogurt
¼ teaspoon cinnamon, ground

1 cup whole wheat flour
2 teaspoons granulated sugar
1 teaspoon baking powder, low sodium
¼ teaspoon baking soda
1 cup fresh blueberries
nonstick cooking spray

INSTRUCTIONS:

Measure the ingredients.

In a small bowl beat the egg with the wet ingredients. Set aside. In a separate bowl combine all dry ingredients. Mix wet into dry and fold in the blueberries.

On a hot, flat surface or a griddle, spray with nonstick cooking spray and pour 1/4 cup of the mixture per portion. As bubbles begin to show, flip the pancake to cook the other side. Remove when pancake is golden.

CATEGORY TAGS:

- O gluten-free
- ◉ high fiber
- O high protein
- O low calorie
- ◉ low carbohydrate / low sugar
- ◉ low cholesterol
- ◉ low fat / low saturated fat
- ◉ low sodium
- O vegan
- ◉ vegetarian
- O whole food plant based
- ◉ whole grain

NUTRITIONAL DATA:

calories	164
fat	3g
sat fat	0.74g
cholesterol	3.9mg
sodium	101mg
carbohydrates	27g
fiber	4g
sugars	8g
protein	7g

Cinnamon, Honey and Vanilla Oatmeal Starter

A lovely thing, oatmeal, credited by the Scottish with helping them survive the cold, hard winters of the Highlands. Hard to say if that is true, but a steady diet of oatmeal in any of its various guises has been shown to help with lowering cholesterol and providing easily digestible complex carbohydrates. Mostly, it's just a good, warm breakfast, and whole grain rolled oats, combined with the flavors of cinnamon, honey and vanilla, are a comforting way to start the day.

PREP INSTRUCTIONS:

Yield: 5 – 6 (¾ cup) servings
Prep Time: 4 minutes

Cooking Time: 7 minutes
Total Time: 11 minutes

RECIPE INGREDIENTS:

1 ½ cups old fashioned rolled oats
1 ½ cups water
1 cup 1% milk
2 ½ tablespoons honey

¾ teaspoon cinnamon
⅛ teaspoon salt
1 teaspoon vanilla extract

INSTRUCTIONS:

Measure the ingredients.

Place liquid ingredients in a sauce pan and bring to a rapid simmer. Add the oatmeal and whisk constantly until oats start to absorb the liquid. Incorporate the rest of the ingredients and lower the heat. Cook until liquid is absorbed. Add water if necessary.

CATEGORY TAGS:

- ◉ gluten-free
- ○ high fiber
- ○ high protein
- ○ low calorie
- ◉ low carbohydrate / low sugar
- ◉ low cholesterol
- ◉ low fat / low saturated fat
- ◉ low sodium
- ○ vegan
- ◉ vegetarian
- ○ whole food plant based
- ◉ whole grain

NUTRITIONAL DATA:

calories	121.50
fat	1.90g
sat fat	0.51g
cholesterol	2.03mg
sodium	59.42mg
carbohydrates	22.97g
fiber	2.17g
sugars	9.27g
protein	3.95g

Quick Brunch Spanish Tortilla

In Mexico, as we've come to learn, the tortilla is a staple corn or flour flatbread, made quick and consumed even quicker. But don't ask for a tortilla to go with your salsa in Spain unless you want this flavorful egg dish—and you just might. The thin Spanish frittata calls for rich flavors and a dense texture courtesy of potatoes, and can be served straight from the oven or cold as a first course.

PREP INSTRUCTIONS:

Yield: 4 Servings
Prep Time: 6 minutes

Cooking Time: 10 minutes
Total Time: 16-20 minutes

RECIPE INGREDIENTS:

5 large eggs
2 teaspoons fresh parsley, chopped
½ cup yellow onion, chopped
¼ teaspoon dried oregano
½ teaspoon kosher salt
⅛ teaspoon ground black pepper
1 ½ cup cooked potatoes, diced

INSTRUCTIONS:

Preheat oven to 350˚F.

Follow the prep technique next to each ingredient.

In a bowl beat the eggs with all the seasonings and fold in the diced potatoes.

Heat an oven-proof skillet on medium heat, spray with nonstick cooking spray and pour in the egg mixture. As the mixture starts to sear, place the skillet in the oven and bake for 8-10 minutes.

CATEGORY TAGS:

- ◉ gluten-free
- ○ high fiber
- ◉ high protein
- ○ low calorie
- ◉ low carbohydrate / low sugar
- ○ low cholesterol
- ○ low fat / low saturated fat
- ○ low sodium
- ○ vegan
- ◉ vegetarian
- ○ whole food plant based
- ○ whole grain

NUTRITIONAL DATA:

calories	119.49
fat	4.83g
sat fat	1.58g
cholesterol	186.00mg
sodium	265.87mg
carbohydrates	11.47g
fiber	1.17g
sugars	1.28g
protein	7.37g

Italian Orange and Cranberry Polenta

Polenta is a grand Italian tradition enjoyed for lunch, dinner and yes, breakfast. Think of the texture of grits, cream of wheat, even oatmeal, then add the nuttiness of cracked corn polenta, low in calories and gluten-free. Cooked until the savory flavors of cranberry, orange and sweet apricot marmalade are soaked into every chewy little grain. Watch the pot carefully while it cooks, and stir often. The reward is a filling and delightful start to the day.

PREP INSTRUCTIONS:

Yield: 4 (3/4 cup) servings
Prep Time: 4 minutes

Cooking Time: 7 minutes
Total Time: 11 minutes

RECIPE INGREDIENTS:

2 cups 1% milk
1 ½ teaspoons honey
1 tablespoon apricot preserve, sugar free
¾ cup polenta, dry, fine
¼ teaspoon kosher salt
3 tablespoons dried cranberries
¼ teaspoon orange extract or 1 teaspoon orange zest

INSTRUCTIONS:

Measure ingredients. Set aside.

Combine wet ingredients together.

In a medium size sauce pan bring milk to a rapid simmer and drizzle the polenta slowly to avoid clumps. Lower heat and add the rest of the ingredients. Whisk constantly until the polenta is cooked through.

CATEGORY TAGS:

- ◉ gluten-free
- ◉ high fiber
- ○ high protein
- ○ low calorie
- ◉ low carbohydrate / low sugar
- ◉ low cholesterol
- ◉ low fat / low saturated fat
- ○ low sodium
- ○ vegan
- ◉ vegetarian
- ○ whole food plant based
- ○ whole grain

NUTRITIONAL DATA:

calories	200
fat	1.27g
sat fat	0.78g
cholesterol	6.10mg
sodium	173.96mg
carbohydrates	41.18g
fiber	3.83g
sugars	11.94g
protein	7.12g

Morning Quinoa and Fruit

Quinoa has become such a salad and side dish staple that we forget the role of this ancient whole grain as a morning meal. Providing a healthy serving of antioxidants and heart-healthy omega-3 fats, the added brown sugar and cinnamon create a wintry oatmeal-like aroma, brown sugar and applesauce for baked apple flavor, and plump dates to add natural sweetness. For textural interest, sprinkle on some toasted almonds or unsalted pistachios.

PREP INSTRUCTIONS:

Yield: 6 (3/4 cup) servings
Prep Time: 3 minutes

Cooking Time: 7 minutes
Total Time: 10 minutes

RECIPE INGREDIENTS:

2 ½ cups soy milk
½ cup unsweetened applesauce
1 cup quinoa, cereal flakes
¼ teaspoon vanilla extract
2 teaspoons raisins
1 ½ tablespoons dates, chopped
1 ½ tablespoons brown sugar
¼ teaspoon ground cinnamon
⅛ teaspoon kosher salt

INSTRUCTIONS:

Measure ingredients and chop the dates. Set aside.

In a saucepan combine the liquid ingredients, bring to a simmer and add the quinoa, stirring slowly.

When the liquid comes back to simmer again, add the rest of the ingredients and stir until nice and creamy.

CATEGORY TAGS:

- ⦿ gluten-free
- ○ high fiber
- ○ high protein
- ○ low calorie
- ⦿ low carbohydrate / low sugar
- ⦿ low cholesterol
- ○ low fat / low saturated fat
- ⦿ low sodium
- ⦿ vegan
- ⦿ vegetarian
- ⦿ whole food plant based
- ⦿ whole grain

NUTRITIONAL DATA:

calories	161
fat	2.80g
sat fat	0.21g
cholesterol	0mg
sodium	95mg
carbohydrates	28g
fiber	2.51g
sugars	14.65g
protein	5.67g

Cumin and Chipotle Spiced Potatoes

A tasty variation of the old standby, home fries. Adding ground cumin and sassy chipotle pepper to sautéed potatoes (small red or waxy Idaho potatoes work best) brings out a great flavor and adds a golden color to the dish. And the richly nutritious potatoes get an added boost from the proven health benefits of cumin, shown to be a good source of iron and an aid to digestion. Rinsing and draining the cut potatoes very well before cooking removes the surface starch and makes for a nice browning in the pan, and be patient—the less you disturb the cooking, the richer the flavor will be.

PREP INSTRUCTIONS:

Yield: 6 (3/4 cup) servings
Prep Time: 5 minutes

Cooking Time: 7 minutes
Total Time: 12 minutes

RECIPE INGREDIENTS:

½ teaspoon olive oil
½ cup yellow onion, diced
½ cup red bell pepper, diced
½ cup green bell pepper, diced
½ teaspoon granulated garlic
¼ teaspoon ground chipotle pepper
½ teaspoon ground cumin
¼ teaspoon kosher salt
4 cups cooked potatoes, diced large

INSTRUCTIONS:

Follow the prep technique next to each ingredient.

In a skillet sauté the onions, peppers, and spices in olive oil. Fold in the cooked potatoes, adding water while sautéing to keep them hot.

CATEGORY TAGS:

- ◉ gluten-free
- ○ high fiber
- ○ high protein
- ○ low calorie
- ◉ low carbohydrate / low sugar
- ◉ low cholesterol
- ◉ low fat / low saturated fat
- ◉ low sodium
- ◉ vegan
- ◉ vegetarian
- ◉ whole food plant based
- ○ whole grain

NUTRITIONAL DATA:

calories	90.10
fat	1.27g
sat fat	0.18g
cholesterol	0mg
sodium	97.80mg
carbohydrates	17.32g
fiber	1.87g
sugars	1.38g
protein	2.67g

Morning Cream of Wheat with Raisins and Coconut

Made from whole wheat semolina, Cream of Wheat was once THE breakfast dish, more popular than oatmeal or packaged cereals. Though not as well known as it once was, it's well worth reviving considering how easy it is to make and how delicious the result can be. Not to mention how good it is for you. High in vitamin D, iron and calcium, a bowl of morning farina can be the basis for a wide variety of breakfast flavors, and in this recipe the addition of raisins, cinnamon and brown sugar bring an almost pie-like savor to the table. Coconut flakes add texture and interest.

PREP INSTRUCTIONS:

Yield: 4 (3/4 cup) servings
Prep Time: 3 minutes

Cooking Time: 6 minutes
Total Time: 9 minutes

RECIPE INGREDIENTS:

1 ½ cups water
1 cup soy milk
½ teaspoon vanilla extract
1 teaspoon brown sugar
¼ cup golden raisins

¼ teaspoon kosher salt
½ teaspoon ground cinnamon
⅔ cup whole-grain Cream of Wheat
2 tablespoons unsweetened coconut flakes
Nonstick cooking spray

INSTRUCTIONS:

Measure the ingredients. Set aside.

In a small saucepan combine water, soy milk and vanilla extract; bring to a simmer.

Add raisins, salt, cinnamon, and brown sugar. Gradually pour in the whole-grain Cream of Wheat and the coconut flakes, stirring constantly until liquid is absorbed.

CATEGORY TAGS:

O gluten-free
◉ high fiber
O high protein
O low calorie
◉ low carbohydrate / low sugar
◉ low cholesterol
◉ low fat / low saturated fat
O low sodium
◉ vegan
◉ vegetarian
◉ whole food plant based
◉ whole grain

NUTRITIONAL DATA:

calories	95
total fat	3g
sat fat	1.71g
cholesterol	0mg
sodium	199mg
carbohydrates	25g
fiber	3g
sugar	7.35g
protein	4.4g

Firm Tofu and Sautéed Peppers Scramble

Pressing firm tofu under a weighted plate guarantees that your scramble won't become a watery mess. Since tofu (low-calorie, high-protein soybean curd) is known to absorb flavors, don't be shy with your seasonings. The combination of earthy turmeric — a spice with great nutritional benefit — and soy sauce heightens the savory nature of tofu and is reminiscent of meat. For a more scrambled egg-like consistency, try using silken tofu instead of firm, or get extra-firm and use instead of ground meat.

PREP INSTRUCTIONS:

Yield: 4 (3/4 cup) servings
Prep Time: 15 minutes

Cooking Time: 15 minutes
Total Time: 30 minutes

RECIPE INGREDIENTS:

14 oz. firm tofu, drained, pressed and cut into small cubes
½ cup yellow onion, diced
¼ cup green bell pepper, diced
¼ cup red bell pepper, diced
1 tablespoon fresh garlic, minced
1 teaspoon garlic powder
1 teaspoon onion powder
¼ teaspoon paprika
¼ teaspoon turmeric
1 tablespoon parsley
1 teaspoon soy sauce, low sodium

INSTRUCTIONS:

Follow the prep technique next to each ingredient.

In a medium bowl combine the tofu with the parsley and spices. In a skillet sprayed with nonstick cooking spray sauté the onion, peppers and garlic. Fold in the tofu mixture and the soy sauce.

Add water if necessary to incorporate all the flavors and cook for 8 to 10 minutes.

CATEGORY TAGS:

- ◉ gluten-free
- ○ high fiber
- ○ high protein
- ○ low calorie
- ◉ low carbohydrate / low sugar
- ◉ low cholesterol
- ○ low fat / low saturated fat
- ◉ low sodium
- ◉ vegan
- ◉ vegetarian
- ◉ whole food plant based
- ○ whole grain

NUTRITIONAL DATA:

calories	100.53
fat	5.15g
sat fat	0.66g
cholesterol	0mg
sodium	51.21mg
carbohydrates	7.36g
fiber	1.29g
sugars	1.58g
protein	9.66g

Pineapple Non-fat Yogurt Smoothie

The original island word for pineapple means "beautiful fruit" and indeed it is. While far more nutritious in its fresh, raw form, frozen pineapple still has great low-fat, high-vitamin C food value. Fun tip: cut the banana into small wheels and freeze for an hour before blending for a richer, thicker smoothie with a texture almost like ice cream.

PREP INSTRUCTIONS:

Yield: 2 (1 cup) servings
Prep Time: 7 minutes

Cooking Time: 0
Total Time: 7 minutes

RECIPE INGREDIENTS:

½ cup pineapple, large dice or chunks
1 tablespoon apricot preserves, sugar free
½ cup soy milk
⅛ teaspoon vanilla extract
¼ cup nonfat Greek yogurt
1 cup banana

INSTRUCTIONS:

Measure the ingredients. Set aside.

In a blender place all the ingredients and blend until smooth.

CATEGORY TAGS:

- ◉ gluten-free
- ◉ high fiber
- ○ high protein
- ○ low calorie
- ○ low carbohydrate / low sugar
- ◉ low cholesterol
- ○ low fat / low saturated fat
- ○ low sodium
- ○ vegan
- ◉ vegetarian
- ○ whole food plant based
- ○ whole grain

NUTRITIONAL DATA:

calories	144.75
fat	1.20g
sat fat	0.16g
cholesterol	0mg
sodium	44.76mg
carbohydrates	31.38g
fiber	3.13g
sugars	23.08g
protein	6.23g

Strawberry Kiwi Morning Smoothie

Here's a secret: the strong flavors of strawberry and kiwi make this smoothie the perfect vehicle for adding kale or spinach to the blender. Try adding a cup of one of these raw greens to this smoothie recipe. The added nutritional boost will help everyone, and the flavor of the greens –disappears – promise! The fuzzy oddities called Kiwis are also known as Chinese gooseberries, but aren't actually gooseberries at all. What they deliver to the sweet smoothie is a low-calorie boost of vitamins C (more than an orange) and K, and a bracing lime-like flavor.

PREP INSTRUCTIONS:

    Yield: 2 (1 cup) servings
    Prep Time: 3 minutes
    Cooking Time: 0 minutes
    Total Time: 3 minutes

RECIPE INGREDIENTS:

    ½ cup frozen strawberries
    1 ½ cups fresh kiwi fruit, peeled and diced
    ½ cup applesauce
    ½ cup banana
    ½ cup ice water

INSTRUCTIONS:

Measure the ingredients. Set aside.

In a blender place all the ingredients and blend until smooth.

CATEGORY TAGS:

- ◉ gluten-free
- ◉ high fiber
- ○ high protein
- ○ low calorie
- ○ low carbohydrate / low sugar
- ◉ low cholesterol
- ◉ low fat / low saturated fat
- ◉ low sodium
- ◉ vegan
- ◉ vegetarian
- ◉ whole food plant based
- ○ whole grain

NUTRITIONAL DATA:

calories	159.08
fat	0.81g
sat fat	0.06g
cholesterol	0g
sodium	6.97mg
carbohydrates	40.23g
fiber	6.32g
sugars	27.56g
protein	2.49g

Almost Instant Three Berry Parfait

So simple it almost takes longer to describe than make. Uncomplicated recipes such as this require the freshest ingredients; check all the berries for ripeness and get an organic, active yogurt with the shortest possible ingredient list. For an added delight, pop the blueberries in the freezer for an hour for a slight crunch and burst of flavor.

PREP INSTRUCTIONS:

Yield: 4 servings
Prep Time: 3 minutes
Cooking Time: 0 minutes
Total Time: 5-7 minutes

RECIPE INGREDIENTS:

4 tablespoons honey oats granola bar, crushed
1 cup fresh strawberries, washed and sliced
½ cup plain nonfat Greek yogurt, divided
½ cup fresh blueberries, washed
½ cup raspberries
1 tablespoon mint, thinly sliced

INSTRUCTIONS:

Follow the prep technique next to each ingredient.

Combine the sliced strawberries with half the yogurt. In 4 separate glasses divide the strawberry mixture and place it on the bottom of each glass. Follow with the blueberries and raspberries. Add the remaining yogurt to each serving and top with the crushed granola bar. Sprinkle with mint and serve.

CATEGORY TAGS:

○ gluten-free
○ high fiber
○ high protein
○ low calorie
◉ low carbohydrate / low sugar
◉ low cholesterol
◉ low fat / low saturated fat
◉ low sodium
○ vegan
◉ vegetarian
○ whole food plant based
○ whole grain

NUTRITIONAL DATA:

calories	107.89
fat	2.30g
sat fat	0.18g
cholesterol	0g
sodium	68.06mg
carbohydrates	18.37g
fiber	2.92g
sugars	9.17g
protein	4.92g

SOUPS & STEWS

Silken Spring Asparagus and Potato Soup

Nothing says spring like the first crop of new asparagus, a sprightly green seasonal crop that has been a favorite since ancient Egypt. There are even asparagus festivals to celebrate its arrival around the world. With antioxidants, vitamins and minerals galore, it is a great base for soup, and this silky smooth recipe adds just enough spices from fresh ginger and good Dijon mustard to bring out its unique flavor. When selecting asparagus, keep in mind that thinner stalks equal younger plants and less chance of encountering a woody stem that needs to be discarded.

PREP INSTRUCTIONS:

Yield: 8 (1 cup) servings
Prep Time: 15 minutes

Cooking Time: 20 minutes
Total Time: 35 minutes

RECIPE INGREDIENTS:

1 ½ teaspoon canola oil
⅓ cup yellow onion, diced
1 ½ teaspoons fresh garlic, chopped
1 teaspoon fresh ginger root, minced
1 cup potato, diced large
5 ½ cups fresh asparagus, cut into 2 inches
4 cups low sodium vegetable broth

½ cup half-and-half
¼ teaspoon kosher salt
¼ cup fresh Italian parsley, chopped
2 ½ teaspoons Dijon mustard
1 teaspoon unsalted butter
½ teaspoon ground black pepper
¼ chives (optional)

INSTRUCTIONS:

Follow the prep technique next to each ingredient.

In a stock pot or large saucepan sauté the ginger, garlic, and onion with canola oil. After onions become translucent add the asparagus, potatoes and vegetable broth. Bring to a simmer and cook until potatoes are soft, about 20 minutes. Remove from the heat and purée soup adding the rest of the ingredients.

Garnish with chives.

CATEGORY TAGS:

- ◉ gluten-free
- ◉ high fiber
- ○ high protein
- ○ low calorie
- ◉ low carbohydrate / low sugar
- ◉ low cholesterol
- ○ low fat / low saturated fat
- ○ low sodium
- ○ vegan
- ◉ vegetarian
- ○ whole food plant based
- ○ whole grain

NUTRITIONAL DATA:

calories	79.47
fat	3.23g
sat fat	1.48g
cholesterol	6.80mg
sodium	180.02mg
carbohydrates	10.60g
fiber	3.10g
sugars	3.89g
protein	3.52g

Three Bean Chili with Corn

So full of flavor and packed with a nutritious trio of beans, colorful and sweet corn, and a generous addition of spices, here's a chili that will sustain the crowd and is a complete meal by itself. The trio of beans adds a healthy portion of protein and fiber. For an extra burst of deep flavor, cook the onions first over moderate heat until they are a rich caramelized brown before adding other ingredients.

PREP INSTRUCTIONS:

Yield: 15 (3/4 cup) servings
Prep Time: 15 minutes

Cooking Time: 20 minutes
Total Time: 35 minutes

RECIPE INGREDIENTS:

1 tablespoon olive oil
2 cups yellow onion, diced
1 ½ green bell pepper, diced
2 tablespoons fresh garlic, minced
1 teaspoon fresh thyme, chopped
2 teaspoons chili powder
1 teaspoon ground cumin
1 tablespoons dried oregano
¾ teaspoon ground chipotle pepper
6 cups, can diced tomatoes in juice

1 cup tomato sauce
1 ¾ cup garbanzos beans, low sodium, drained and rinsed
1 ¾ cup black beans, low sodium, drained and rinsed
1 ¾ cup pinto beans, low sodium, drained and rinsed
1 ½ cup sweet corn, drained
1 teaspoon kosher salt
1 cup water
¼ cup cilantro, chopped
½ cup fresh parsley, chopped

INSTRUCTIONS:

Follow the prep technique next to each ingredient.

In a large pot, sauté onions, garlic and green peppers with the herbs and spices. Fold in the tomato product and mix well. Add the beans, salt, and water. Cover and simmer until flavors are well blended, about 20 to 25 minutes. Garnish with the fresh herbs.

CATEGORY TAGS:

- ◉ gluten-free
- ◉ high fiber
- ○ high protein
- ○ low calorie
- ◉ low carbohydrate / low sugar
- ◉ low cholesterol
- ◉ low fat / low saturated fat
- ○ low sodium
- ◉ vegan
- ◉ vegetarian
- ◉ whole food plant based
- ○ whole grain

NUTRITIONAL DATA:

calories	136.41
fat	2.49g
sat fat	0.28g
cholesterol	0mg
sodium	624.69mg
carbohydrates	23.73g
fiber	7.60g
sugars	3.27g
protein	6.42g

Chicken Noodle and Vegetable Soup

The classic "Mother's penicillin" with more than a hint of truth. There really is some evidence to show that classic chicken soup may act as an anti-inflammatory, and slow the development of upper respiratory cold symptoms. But there's no reason to wait until cold season to enjoy the comforting aroma and taste of this rich soup, and it's fun to experiment with different sizes of noodles (kids love the really thin ones) and there are some tasty gluten-free options available.

PREP INSTRUCTIONS:

Yield: 8 (1 cup) servings
Prep Time: 10 minutes

Cooking Time: 20 minutes
Total Time: 30 minutes

RECIPE INGREDIENTS:

1 tablespoon cornstarch
6 cups low sodium chicken broth
6 oz. chicken breast raw, cut into chunks
¾ cup carrots, diced
¾ cup yellow onion, diced
1 cup celery, diced

⅛ teaspoon ground bay leaf
⅛ teaspoon ground cayenne pepper
½ teaspoon kosher salt
½ cup egg noodles
¼ cup parsley

INSTRUCTIONS:

Follow the prep technique next to each ingredient.

In a medium saucepan sauté the onions, celery, carrots, and spices in a 1/2 cup of water or broth. After onions are translucent, add the diced chicken and sear. Add the broth and bring to a soft boil over medium heat; fold in the noodles. Make a slurry with the cornstarch, adding 3 tablespoons of water or broth; add to the soup and simmer for 15 to 20 minutes.

CATEGORY TAGS:

- ○ gluten-free
- ○ high fiber
- ○ high protein
- ○ low calorie
- ◉ low carbohydrate / low sugar
- ○ low cholesterol
- ◉ low fat / low saturated fat
- ○ low sodium
- ○ vegan
- ○ vegetarian
- ○ whole food plant based
- ○ whole grain

NUTRITIONAL DATA:

calories	137.99
fat	3.02g
sat fat	0.94g
cholesterol	30.58mg
sodium	412.57mg
carbohydrates	16.28g
fiber	1.19g
sugars	4.55g
protein	11.15g

Moroccan Spiced Pumpkin Soup

Cinnamon, allspice, coriander, pepper. The exotic flavors of Morocco, so highly prized that they have been used as currency and impelled Europe's exploration of the entire world. The fact that they all have well-documented health benefits is an added bonus. The subtle flavor of allspice is an ideal match for fresh pumpkin and brings out the sweetness and richness. Ground coriander adds an earthy, nutty flavor—if you're not fond of the taste, substitute cumin and a touch of ground fennel seed.

PREP INSTRUCTIONS:

Yield: 8 (1 cup) servings
Prep Time: 10 minutes

Cooking Time: 25 minutes
Total Time: 35 minutes

RECIPE INGREDIENTS:

1 ½ teaspoons canola oil
2 ½ cups yellow onion, diced
⅛ teaspoon cinnamon
1/16 teaspoon or a pinch of ground allspice
⅛ teaspoon ground cayenne pepper

⅛ teaspoon black ground pepper
¼ teaspoon ground coriander
4 cups fresh pumpkin, peeled, clean and diced
3 cups low sodium vegetable broth
¼ cup 1% milk

INSTRUCTIONS:

Follow the prep technique next to each ingredient.

In a stock pot, sauté onions in oil until translucent. Add the spices and diced pumpkin, and sauté to extract their aroma. Cook over medium heat until pumpkin is tender, add the milk and turn off heat. Purée soup and turn heat back on, cook for five more minutes. Remove from heat and serve.

CATEGORY TAGS:

- ◉ gluten-free
- ○ high fiber
- ○ high protein
- ○ low calorie
- ◉ low carbohydrate / low sugar
- ◉ low cholesterol
- ◉ low fat / low saturated fat
- ◉ low sodium
- ○ vegan
- ◉ vegetarian
- ○ whole food plant based
- ○ whole grain

NUTRITIONAL DATA:

calories	54.03
fat	1.07g
sat fat	0.17g
cholesterol	0.38mg
sodium	58.48mg
carbohydrates	10.43g
fiber	1.58g
sugars	4.86g
protein	1.78g

Bombay Sweet Potato Chicken Curry

Take a walk through neighborhood streets in southern India and the air will be sweet with the smell of curry, like this flavorful creation. The spice blend we call curry isn't a traditional thing at all (the word "curry" means sauce) but an invention of Colonial Britain: curry dishes vary widely as you travel from regions of India to Indonesia to Japan. To get a more authentic flavor, mash the garlic and ginger together into a paste before cooking, and very briefly heat the dry spices in oil (called "blooming") before adding other ingredients.

PREP INSTRUCTIONS:

Yield: 8 (1 cup) servings
Prep Time: 10 minutes

Cooking Time: 25 minutes
Total Time: 35 minutes

RECIPE INGREDIENTS:

1 tablespoon olive oil
¾ cup yellow onion, diced
1 teaspoon fresh garlic, chopped
1 teaspoon fresh ginger root, minced
¼ teaspoon red crushed pepper flakes
¾ tablespoon curry powder
1 ¼ teaspoons ground coriander
1 ¼ teaspoons ground turmeric
½ teaspoon kosher salt

½ teaspoon ground black pepper
6 oz. raw chicken, chopped
1 cup low sodium vegetable broth
4 cups canned diced tomatoes in juice
1 ½ cups sweet potato, diced
½ cup garbanzos, drained and rinsed
½ cup frozen peas
1 tablespoon lemon juice

INSTRUCTIONS:

Follow the prep technique next to each ingredient.

In a medium stock pot, add the olive oil, onions, garlic and spices and sauté for 3 to 5 minutes at medium heat. Add chicken and sear. Bring heat to high, and add the broth, potatoes, tomatoes, and garbanzos. Cover and lower heat to simmer. Cook approximately 15 to 20 minutes. Add peas and lemon juice, cook for 5 more minutes before removing from heat.

CATEGORY TAGS:

- ◉ gluten-free
- ◉ high fiber
- ○ high protein
- ○ low calorie
- ◉ low carbohydrate / low sugar
- ◉ low cholesterol
- ◉ low fat / low saturated fat
- ○ low sodium
- ○ vegan
- ○ vegetarian
- ○ whole food plant based
- ○ whole grain

NUTRITIONAL DATA:

calories	122.93
fat	2.64g
sat fat	0.51g
cholesterol	14.24mg
sodium	497.39mg
carbohydrates	17.16g
fiber	4.73g
sugars	4.44g
protein	7.99g

Tuscan Bean Stew

Here's a bright and flavorful stew with an Italian flair. Cooks in Tuscany traditionally slow-cook beans in a clay pot called a fagioliera, a vessel that became popular after Columbus brought beans to Europe from the Americas, along with tomatoes and potatoes. So this is actually a New World recipe! There's no need to clean up a clay pot; stovetop cooking will bring out these marvelous flavors just as well. More beans and vegetables can be added to leftovers (if there are any) for a delicious never-ending soup.

PREP INSTRUCTIONS:

Yield: 8 (1 cup) servings
Prep Time: 10 minutes

Cooking Time: 25 minutes
Total Time: 35 minutes

RECIPE INGREDIENTS:

2 cups yellow onions, diced
¼ cup carrots, diced
1 tablespoon fresh rosemary, minced
¼ teaspoon ground bay leaf
1 tablespoon dried oregano
2 tablespoons tomato paste
½ teaspoon kosher salt
1 tablespoon ground paprika

¼ teaspoon crushed red chili flakes
2 cups, can diced tomatoes in juice
½ cup kidney beans, drained and rinsed
1 cup garbanzos, drained and rinsed
1 cup cannellini beans, drained and rinsed
2 cups low sodium vegetable broth
¼ cup parsley, chopped

INSTRUCTIONS:

Follow the prep technique next to each ingredient.

In a stock pot, sauté the onions and carrots with the herbs and spices in a little water to create steam and release their flavor. Fold in the tomatoes, beans, and broth, and bring to a soft boil for 5 minutes. Lower to simmer and cook 20 to 25 minutes. Remove from heat and add fresh parsley.

CATEGORY TAGS:

- ◉ gluten-free
- ◉ high fiber
- ○ high protein
- ○ low calorie
- ◉ low carbohydrate / low sugar
- ◉ low cholesterol
- ◉ low fat / low saturated fat
- ○ low sodium
- ◉ vegan
- ◉ vegetarian
- ◉ whole food plant based
- ○ whole grain

NUTRITIONAL DATA:

calories	125.18
fat	0.96g
sat fat	0.13g
cholesterol	0mg
sodium	488.82mg
carbohydrates	23.17g
fiber	7.72g
sugars	4.98g
protein	6.42g

Andalucian-Spiced Garbanzo Stew

Flavors of Andalucía by way of Portugal and North Africa infuse this simple chickpea stew with exotic tastes and aromas. With high protein and fiber content, and exceptional levels of iron, magnesium and amino acids, chickpeas are a near-perfect low-cholesterol food. No need to soak beans or grind spices when even the most available ingredients result in a flavorful and filling dish that is easily customizable to your tastes. Use smoky or sweet paprika, spicier mixes of chili powder, or add chopped fresh tomatoes or a few handfuls of fresh spinach and a squeeze of lemon to create a new dish every time.

PREP INSTRUCTIONS:

Yield: 7 (1 cup) servings
Prep Time: 7 minutes

Cooking Time: 15 minutes
Total Time: 22 minutes

RECIPE INGREDIENTS:

1 tablespoon olive oil
½ cup sofrito (page 184)
2 tablespoons tomato paste
⅛ teaspoon ground cumin or 1 bay leaf
2 (28 oz) cans garbanzo beans, low sodium
¾ teaspoon fresh garlic, chopped

1 ½ teaspoons paprika
1 ½ teaspoons chili powder
1 teaspoon ground cumin
2 teaspoons dried oregano
¼ cup fresh cilantro, chopped

INSTRUCTIONS:

Follow the prep technique next to each ingredient.

In a stock pot over medium heat sauté sofrito in olive oil with the garlic, oregano, bay leaf, and tomato paste. Add garbanzo beans and fold in the spices. Simmer on moderate heat for 20 minutes. Remove from heat and fold in the chopped cilantro.

CATEGORY TAGS:

- ◉ gluten-free
- ◉ high fiber
- ○ high protein
- ○ low calorie
- ○ low carbohydrate / low sugar
- ◉ low cholesterol
- ○ low fat / low saturated fat
- ○ low sodium
- ◉ vegan
- ◉ vegetarian
- ◉ whole food plant based
- ○ whole grain

NUTRITIONAL DATA:

calories	230
fat	7g
sat fat	0.79g
cholesterol	0mg
sodium	341mg
carbohydrates	34g
fiber	11.12g
sugars	7g
protein	12g

Slow Simmered Chicken Fricassee with Carrot and Potato

Fricassee is an odd word for a rather sophisticated cooking process that dates back centuries and which, with a little bit of effort, produces an amazing result. Building upon the base of peppers, onions, garlic and aromatic herbs, chicken is first sautéed to release juices and build that wonderful flavor that only comes from browning in a pan, then braised over low, moist heat to incorporate all the wonderful flavors into the meat and tenderize each ingredient. This healthy preparation adds flavor instead of fat and sodium.

PREP INSTRUCTIONS:

Yield: 15 (1 ¾ cup) servings
Prep Time: 20 minutes

Cooking Time: 40 minutes
Total Time: 60 minutes

RECIPE INGREDIENTS:

¼ cup olive oil
½ cup yellow onion, diced
¼ cup pimientos, drained and diced
½ cup sofrito (page 184)
½ tablespoon fresh thyme, chopped
1 ½ tablespoons dried oregano
1 ½ tablespoons ground cumin
1 teaspoon paprika
1 tablespoon chili powder

¾ cup tomato sauce
2 bay leaves
48 oz. fresh chicken breast, cut into large chunks
1 ½ lbs. = 4 cups russet potatoes, chopped
12 oz. = 2 cups carrot, diced large
1 ½ teaspoon kosher salt
1 quart low sodium chicken broth
¼ cup cilantro (optional)

INSTRUCTIONS:

Follow the prep technique next to each ingredient.

In a stock pot add the olive oil and sauté the onions, sofrito, pimiento pepper, herbs and spices. Add chicken and sear, then add the tomato sauce. Add the potatoes and chicken broth. Simmer over medium heat until softly boiling, then cover and lower heat to medium low. Cook for 30 to 40 minutes. Remove from heat and serve with cilantro.

CATEGORY TAGS:

- ◉ gluten-free
- ○ high fiber
- ○ high protein
- ○ low calorie
- ◉ low carbohydrate / low sugar
- ○ low cholesterol
- ○ low fat / low saturated fat
- ○ low sodium
- ○ vegan
- ○ vegetarian
- ○ whole food plant based
- ○ whole grain

NUTRITIONAL DATA:

calories	184
fat	6g
sat fat	1g
cholesterol	61mg
sodium	510mg
carbohydrates	12g
fiber	2.5g
sugars	3g
protein	23g

Italian Bean, Vegetable, and Pasta Stew

Pasta fagioli (pronounced "fah-ZHOO-lee") literally means "pasta and beans", and is a traditional stew/soup of Italy and Sicily. Traditionally made with short tube-like ditalini pasta, it is very forgiving of style and requires just a "macaroni" type pasta. And feel free to use any canned beans available—Italians typically add white cannellini or the lovely pink cranberry beans they call borlotti, but any beans other than seasoned black beans will work. The combination of proteins in the beans and pasta, along with the squash and potatoes, makes this a complete meal.

PREP INSTRUCTIONS:

Yield: 8 (1 cup) servings
Prep Time: 20 minutes

Cooking Time: 25 minutes
Total Time: 45 minutes

RECIPE INGREDIENTS:

1 ½ tablespoons olive oil
½ cup celery, diced
½ cup yellow onion, diced
1 teaspoon fresh garlic, minced
⅓ cup carrots, diced
1 bay leaf
⅛ black pepper
¾ cup potato, chopped
½ cup dry pasta shells

½ cup butternut squash, chopped
2 cups northern beans, drained and rinsed
1 ½ cups, fresh tomatoes, diced
2 ½ cups low sodium vegetable broth
¼ cup green onion, chopped
¾ cup green beans, snipped and cut 1 inch long
¾ cup zucchini squash, chopped
¼ cup fresh basil, shredded

INSTRUCTIONS:

Follow the prep technique next to each ingredient.

In a medium size stock pot add olive oil and sauté the celery, onions, carrots, garlic and bay leaf. Fold in the potatoes, butternut squash, green beans, pasta, northern beans and tomatoes with the vegetable broth. Bring the soup to a gentle boil, cover and lower the heat to a low simmer, cook for 15 minutes. Add the rest of the ingredients and simmer until squash is tender but firm.

CATEGORY TAGS:

- O gluten-free
- ◉ high fiber
- O high protein
- O low calorie
- ◉ low carbohydrate / low sugar
- ◉ low cholesterol
- ◉ low fat / low saturated fat
- O low sodium
- ◉ vegan
- ◉ vegetarian
- O whole food plant based
- O whole grain

NUTRITIONAL DATA:

calories	135.47
fat	3.32g
sat fat	0.41g
cholesterol	0mg
sodium	154.91mg
carbohydrates	22.39g
fiber	5.99g
sugars	4.56g
protein	4.53g

SALADS

Roasted Beet, Kale and Pepper Salad

A perfect side salad to keep in the fridge for family events or last-minute picnics, and a colorful one at that. Roasted beets, high in potassium, magnesium and vitamin A, turn tender and sweet in the oven. If you can buy them complete with tops, add those luscious greens to the salad. Oranges and peppers make a satisfying, tangy crunch when mixed together, and kale, rich in iron, comes alive in the presence of citrus juice. Boosted by a generous helping of whole grain bulgur, this salad will delight.

PREP INSTRUCTIONS:

Yield: 14 (3/4 cup) servings
Prep Time: 20 minutes

Cooking Time: 45 minutes
Total Time: 65 minutes

RECIPE INGREDIENTS:

1 lb. beets
1 cup bulgur wheat, dry
1 ¾ cups boiling water
2 cups oranges, sectioned and cut into small chunks
3 cups fresh kale, stems removed
½ cup shallots, chopped
½ cup red bell pepper, diced
½ cup yellow bell pepper, diced

¼ cup walnuts, toasted and chopped
⅓ cup golden balsamic vinegar
⅓ cup freshly squeezed orange juice
1 tablespoon olive oil
2 teaspoons fresh thyme, minced
¾ teaspoon ground black pepper
½ teaspoon salt

INSTRUCTIONS:

Follow the prep technique next to each ingredient. Preheat oven at 350°F.

Wash and cut beets, place in a baking pan. Add enough water to cover the beets nearly halfway then cover with foil. Bake for 45 to 60 minutes. Let stand uncovered, remove the skins and dice the beets into small pieces. Meanwhile place the bulgur wheat in a small container, add the boiling water, and cover. Let stand for five to seven minutes. Uncover and fluff with a fork. Cool down completely.

Add ¼ cup water to a small pot with a lid and steam kale until bright green, approximately 3-5 minutes. Remove from heat, drain and cool down, cut into medium bite size. Make the vinaigrette with the olive oil, orange juice, golden balsamic, thyme, salt and pepper. In a large bowl, fold all the ingredients together and add vinaigrette.

CATEGORY TAGS:

O gluten-free
O high fiber
O high protein
O low calorie
◉ low carbohydrate / low sugar
◉ low cholesterol
◉ low fat / low saturated fat
◉ low sodium
◉ vegan
◉ vegetarian
◉ whole food plant based
◉ whole grain

NUTRITIONAL DATA:

calories	90.92
fat	2.61gg
sat fat	0.30g
cholesterol	0mg
sodium	100.95mg
carbohydrates	15.43g
fiber	2.74g
sugars	5.96g
protein	3.12g

Crisp "Almost Pickled" Cucumber Salad

The long, thin cucumber called either English, hothouse or seedless (there really are seeds, but they're tiny and edible) is the one to find, both for ease of use and sweeter taste. It is usually offered wrapped in plastic, which eliminates the need for waxing, another bonus. This recipe is what might be termed an "almost pickle", a 20-minute soak in two kinds of vinegar bringing the cuke to a softened and slightly tart state without calling for cooking or an unbearably long wait before eating this refreshing salad.

PREP INSTRUCTIONS:

Yield: 8 (3/4 cup) servings
Prep Time: 20 minutes

Cooking Time: 0 minutes
Total Time: 20 minutes

RECIPE INGREDIENTS:

1 teaspoon olive oil
1 tablespoon balsamic vinegar
1 tablespoon red wine vinegar
1 teaspoon fresh garlic, minced
⅛ teaspoon kosher salt
⅛ teaspoon ground black pepper

½ to 1 tablespoon fresh oregano, minced
¼ cup red onions, diced
1 ¾ cups plum tomatoes, chopped
1 ¾ cups English cucumber, chopped
¼ cup fresh basil, julienned

INSTRUCTIONS:

Follow the prep technique next to each ingredient.

In a small bowl make vinaigrette with the oil, vinegars, garlic, salt, pepper and oregano. In a medium bowl combine the rest of the ingredients, fold in the vinaigrette and the fresh basil.

Chill and serve.

CATEGORY TAGS:

- ◉ gluten-free
- ○ high fiber
- ○ high protein
- ◉ low calorie
- ◉ low carbohydrate / low sugar
- ◉ low cholesterol
- ◉ low fat / low saturated fat
- ◉ low sodium
- ◉ vegan
- ◉ vegetarian
- ◉ whole food plant based
- ○ whole grain

NUTRITIONAL DATA:

calories	27.30
fat	0.71g
sat fat	0.10g
cholesterol	0mg
sodium	33.15mg
carbohydrates	4.68g
fiber	1.37g
sugars	2.91g
protein	1.19g

Crisp and Bold Jicama-Apple Salad with Garlic Vinaigrette

Crunch, bold and subtle flavors, and a great alternative to a standard salad. Worthy of side dish status, this picnic picker-upper combines crisp jicama (pronounced HEE-cama) matchsticks and juicy apples (try using tart green Granny Smiths or crisp sweet Galas) with the chew of sharp cranberries and toasted walnuts. Along with a generous serving of spinach, it is packed with nutrition, made even more attractive by the exuberant amount of garlic and savory tastes of Worcestershire and apple cider vinegar in the dressing.

PREP INSTRUCTIONS:

Yield: 4 servings
Prep Time: 15 minutes

Cooking Time: 0
Total Time: 15 minutes

RECIPE INGREDIENTS:

6 cups baby spinach
½ cup apple, julienned or into matchsticks
2 cups jicama, julienned

⅓ cup cranberries, dried
6 tablespoons, Sweet Garlic Dressing (see below)

For the Sweet Garlic Dressing: Yield: 21 (1 ½ tablespoons) servings

¼ cup water
½ cup apple cider vinegar
¼ cup canola oil
½ cup granulated sugar
¼ red onion

4- 5 cloves of garlic
1 teaspoon Worcestershire sauce
¼ teaspoon salt
1 teaspoon ground black pepper

INSTRUCTIONS:

Follow the prep technique next to each ingredient.

For the dressing: Mix vinegar, oil and sugar. Pour a small amount of mixture into the blender, add salt, pepper, Worcestershire, garlic and onion, then purée. Add the remaining vinegar mixture. Chill.

In a medium bowl combine apples and jicama with the dressing (to avoid oxidation). Fold all ingredients together with the above and serve. Top with toasted walnuts.

CATEGORY TAGS:

- ◉ gluten-free
- ◉ high fiber
- ○ high protein
- ○ low calorie
- ◉ low carbohydrate / low sugar
- ◉ low cholesterol
- ○ low fat / low saturated fat
- ◉ low sodium
- ○ vegan
- ○ vegetarian
- ○ whole food plant based
- ○ whole grain

NUTRITIONAL DATA:

calories	157.04
fat	5.25g
sat fat	0.48g
cholesterol	0.01mg
sodium	97.96mg
carbohydrates	25.52g
fiber	6.10g
sugars	15.66g
protein	3.13g

Crunchy Jicama, Cabbage and Pineapple Slaw

Here's a bright and refreshing change from cole slaw or carrot salad, mixing the snap of jicama, carrots and red pepper to thin shreds of napa cabbage for a low-fat, low-sodium side dish. An unexpected sweetness comes from mini bits of pineapple, all of it dressed in a mayonnaise base enlivened by honey, garlic and ginger.

PREP INSTRUCTIONS:

Yield: 16 (3/4 cup) servings
Prep Time: 30 minutes

Cooking Time: 0
Total Time: 30 minutes

RECIPE INGREDIENTS:

4 cups napa cabbage, shredded
3 cups jicama, julienned
2 cups red bell pepper, julienned
1 cup carrot, julienned
2 cups fresh pineapple, diced
2 tablespoon fresh garlic, minced

1 teaspoon fresh ginger, minced
¼ cup lime juice
2 tablespoons honey
⅓ cup light mayonnaise
⅛ teaspoon cayenne pepper

INSTRUCTIONS:

Follow the prep technique next to each ingredient.

In a large bowl combine the napa cabbage, jicama, red bell pepper, carrots and pineapple. Mix well.

Combine the ginger, garlic, lime juice, honey, light mayonnaise and the cayenne to make the dressing.

Fold dressing into the mixture thirty minutes prior to serving.

CATEGORY TAGS:

- ◉ gluten-free
- ○ high fiber
- ○ high protein
- ○ low calorie
- ◉ low carbohydrate / low sugar
- ◉ low cholesterol
- ◉ low fat / low saturated fat
- ◉ low sodium
- ○ vegan
- ◉ vegetarian
- ○ whole food plant based
- ○ whole grain

NUTRITIONAL DATA:

calories	55.22
fat	1.74g
sat fat	0.24g
cholesterol	1.56mg
sodium	37.24mg
carbohydrates	9.12g
fiber	1.77g
sugars	5.14g
protein	0.79g

Low Fat Tomato, Olive and Chickpea Greek Salad

A classic salad made simple. While it may seem like the item called "Greek salad", hero of diner menus from coast to coast, must be an American invention, the combination of onion, tomato, cucumber, pepper and olives actually has been enjoyed on tables in Greece for decades, where it is called a "country salad". In this version the standard, very salty feta cheese has been replaced with far healthier garbanzo beans for a lighter taste. The dressing, a light and tart lemon vinaigrette laced with honey and oregano, is true to its Grecian roots.

PREP INSTRUCTIONS:

Yield: 6 servings
Prep Time: 20 minutes

Cooking Time: 0
Total Time: 20 minutes

RECIPE INGREDIENTS:

8 cups romaine lettuce, cut into bite size
½ red onion, julienned
3 plum tomatoes, cut into slices
1 green bell pepper, julienned

½ English cucumber, cut half lengthwise, then sliced
¼ cup black Kalamata olive, sliced
¾ cup garbanzos beans, drained and rinsed

For the Vinaigrette:
2 teaspoons fresh garlic, minced
¼ cup lemon juice
¼ cup red wine vinegar
2 ½ tablespoons olive oil

1 tablespoon honey
1 ½ teaspoons fresh oregano, minced
½ teaspoon ground black pepper
Pinch salt (optional)

INSTRUCTIONS:

Follow the prep technique next to each ingredient.

In a small bowl combine the ingredients for the vinaigrette, mix well. Set aside.

Chop romaine into bite size. Slice the red onion, plum tomatoes, green pepper and cucumber. In a salad bowl combine vegetables with the garbanzos and olives. Fold in the dressing and serve.

CATEGORY TAGS:

- ◉ gluten-free
- ◉ high fiber
- ○ high protein
- ○ low calorie
- ◉ low carbohydrate / low sugar
- ◉ low cholesterol
- ◉ low fat / low saturated fat
- ◉ low sodium
- ○ vegan
- ◉ vegetarian
- ◉ whole food plant based
- ○ whole grain

NUTRITIONAL DATA:

calories	121
fat	6.5g
sat fat	1g
cholesterol	0mg
sodium	89mg
carbohydrates	14.5g
fiber	4g
sugars	6.69g
protein	3.26g

Fresh Garden Lentil Salad with Feta and Mint

With a package of dry lentils in the cupboard, dinner is always just a few minutes away. These highly versatile legumes add heart-healthy folates and magnesium to your diet, along with an energy boost of protein and complex carbohydrates. Lentils come in a wide variety of colors, flavors and sizes. The lentils in this salad are cooked to just doneness, and hold up well when mixed with onion, tomato and cucumber and the salty tang of crumbled feta cheese.

PREP INSTRUCTIONS:

Yield: 6 (3/4 cup) servings   Cooking Time: 15 minutes
Prep Time: 15 minutes   Total Time: 30 minutes

RECIPE INGREDIENTS:

1 cup lentils, dry   2 tablespoons shallot, diced
¼ yellow onion   1 ½ teaspoons olive oil
1 bay leaf   1 ½ tablespoons lemon juice
1 ½ cups water   1 tablespoon fresh mint, chopped
2 plum tomatoes, chopped   2 tablespoons feta cheese
1 cup English cucumber, chopped

INSTRUCTIONS:

Follow the prep technique next to each ingredient.

Place lentils, bay leaf, yellow onions and water into a saucepan. Bring to a boil and reduce the heat to medium low. Cook lentils for 15 to 20 minutes or until tender but firm.

Drain lentils and remove the onion and the bay leaf. Place lentils on a cookie sheet and cool completely.

Transfer the lentils to a medium size bowl and fold in the rest of the ingredients.

CATEGORY TAGS:

- ◉ gluten-free
- ◉ high fiber
- ○ high protein
- ○ low calorie
- ◉ low carbohydrate / low sugar
- ◉ low cholesterol
- ◉ low fat / low saturated fat
- ◉ low sodium
- ○ vegan
- ◉ vegetarian
- ○ whole food plant based
- ○ whole grain

NUTRITIONAL DATA:

calories	143.54
fat	2.27g
sat fat	0.70g
cholesterol	2.78mg
sodium	34.97mg
carbohydrates	23.19g
fiber	4.14g
sugars	2.36g
protein	8.85g

Mediterranean Parsley and Bulgur Wheat Tabbouleh Salad

The rising popularity of tabbouleh proves that good food connects with people. This Middle Eastern salad is claimed by many different lands as their own, but whether it's the Lebanese (less wheat, more spices), Turkish (added pomegranate and tomato paste) or Armenian (no mint, added cucumber) varieties, this parsley salad is a delightful main course, side dish or pita filling. The combination of masses of iron-rich parsley and high fiber whole grain wheat is the epitome of the Mediterranean diet. For those with gluten limitations, a tasty variation can be made using quinoa instead of bulgur.

PREP INSTRUCTIONS:

Yield: 6 (1/2 cup) servings
Prep Time: 8 minutes

Cooking Time: 6 minutes
Total Time: 14 minutes

RECIPE INGREDIENTS:

½ cup bulgur wheat
½ cup boiling water
½ cup Italian parsley, chopped
½ tablespoon green onions, thinly sliced
2 plum tomatoes, diced
1 tablespoon fresh mint, chopped

2 teaspoon fresh garlic, minced
½ teaspoon olive oil
2 tablespoons lemon juice
⅛ teaspoon kosher salt
¼ teaspoon black pepper

INSTRUCTIONS:

Follow the prep technique next to each ingredient.

In a small bowl combine boiling water and bulgur wheat. Cover with plastic for 5 minutes or until water is absorbed; fluff with a fork and cool completely. Combine the rest of the salad ingredients and fold in the cooked bulgur wheat. Keep refrigerated.

CATEGORY TAGS:

○ gluten-free
○ high fiber
○ high protein
○ low calorie
◉ low carbohydrate / low sugar
◉ low cholesterol
◉ low fat / low saturated fat
◉ low sodium
◉ vegan
◉ vegetarian
◉ whole food plant based
◉ whole grain

NUTRITIONAL DATA:

calories	52.06
fat	0.65g
sat fat	0.10g
cholesterol	0mg
sodium	46.84mg
carbohydrates	10.81g
fiber	2.01g
sugars	0.78g
protein	1.89g

Summer Scallion Vegetable Slaw

The surprising addition of fresh pear lifts the flavor profile of this salad from cole slaw into a special dish. With more research pointing towards the benefits of cruciferous vegetables, a serving of this cabbage-rich salad will help your heart, cholesterol and overall health – and it is a tasty way to deliver good nutrition. The dressing is a uniquely Asian combination of sweet, hot, salty and sour that can be used at many other meals. Bright green soybean edamame can be found precooked in your grocer's freezer section.

PREP INSTRUCTIONS:

Yield: 4 servings
Prep Time: 15 minutes

Cooking Time: 0
Total Time: 15 minutes

RECIPE INGREDIENTS:

3 cups red cabbage, shredded
3 cups green cabbage, shredded
1 cup red bell pepper, thinly sliced
1 cup edamame beans, cooked and cooled

1 cup fresh carrot, julienned
1 cup scallions, ½ inch bias cut
½ pear, thinly sliced

For the Vinaigrette Dressing:
½ cup rice vinegar
1 tablespoon fresh ginger, minced
1 tablespoon fresh garlic, minced

2 tablespoon shallots, minced
2 teaspoons soy sauce
1 teaspoon sesame oil

INSTRUCTIONS:

Follow the prep technique next to each ingredient.

Combine all ingredients for dressing and blend well.

In a large bowl combine salad ingredients and fold in the dressing. Refrigerate at least 10 to 15 minutes before serving.

CATEGORY TAGS:

- ● gluten-free
- ● high fiber
- ○ high protein
- ○ low calorie
- ● low carbohydrate / low sugar
- ● low cholesterol
- ○ low fat / low saturated fat
- ○ low sodium
- ● vegan
- ● vegetarian
- ● whole food plant based
- ○ whole grain

NUTRITIONAL DATA:

calories	127
fat	3g
sat fat	0.21g
cholesterol	0mg
sodium	150mg
carbohydrates	21g
fiber	7g
sugars	10g
protein	6g

APPETIZERS & SIDES

Jerusalem Couscous with Cinnamon Ginger

Pearl, or Israeli, couscous has much larger pieces of pasta than the more familiar style, and brings an interesting texture to a very easy-to-make dish. Adding ginger and cinnamon to apricots gives them an earthy, almost dessert-like flavor and would complement a turkey or duck main course. For a toastier flavor, add the couscous to the dry sauce pan to brown for about a minute before adding the broth—but watch carefully!

PREP INSTRUCTIONS:

Yield: 4 (1/2 cup) servings
Prep Time: 5 minutes

Cooking Time: 10 minutes
Total Time: 15 minutes

RECIPE INGREDIENTS:

1 ¼ cups vegetable broth, low sodium
1 cup Israeli couscous, dry
4 tablespoons dried apricot, chopped
2 teaspoons fresh ginger, minced
⅛ teaspoon ground cinnamon

⅛ teaspoon kosher salt
1 ½ tablespoons red bell pepper, diced
1 ½ tablespoons yellow pepper, diced
1 tablespoon Italian parsley, chopped
Optional garnish: Toasted almonds

INSTRUCTIONS:

Follow the prep technique next to each ingredient.

In a small sauce pan bring vegetable broth to a boil. Stir in couscous, salt and ginger; bring back to a boil and cover. Low simmer for 8-10 minutes. Remove from heat and fluff. Add apricots, peppers, parsley and cinnamon. Serve and garnish with toasted almonds.

CATEGORY TAGS:

- ○ gluten-free
- ○ high fiber
- ○ high protein
- ○ low calorie
- ○ low carbohydrate / low sugar
- ◉ low cholesterol
- ◉ low fat / low saturated fat
- ◉ low sodium
- ◉ vegan
- ◉ vegetarian
- ○ whole food plant based
- ○ whole grain

NUTRITIONAL DATA:

calories	160.47
fat	0.03g
sat fat	0.01g
cholesterol	0mg
sodium	106.52mg
carbohydrates	34.59g
fiber	2.80g
sugars	2.80g
protein	4.40g

Tunisian Vegetarian Medley with Rustic Quinoa

Those unfamiliar with harissa will be delighted by this North African condiment. There are as many different recipes for this ubiquitous Tunisian seasoning. Cumin, coriander, garlic and spicy peppers are required ingredients. Some like it smoky (add paprika), some sweet (roasted red pepper), and some double up on the cayenne for a palate-awakening hit of spice.

PREP INSTRUCTIONS:

Yield: 10 (3/4 cup) servings
Prep Time: 10 minutes

Cooking Time: 20 minutes
Total Time: 30 minutes

RECIPE INGREDIENTS:

1 ½ cups quinoa, uncooked
3 cups water
1 tablespoon olive oil
1 cup yellow squash, chopped
1 cup zucchini squash, chopped
1 ½ cups eggplant, chopped
1 whole red bell pepper, chopped
2 plum tomatoes, chopped

¼ teaspoon ground black pepper
¼ teaspoon ground cumin
¼ teaspoon coriander
½ teaspoon granulated garlic
¼ teaspoon kosher salt
1 tablespoon fresh parsley
Water as needed for sautéing
1 serving Harissa, recipe follows

Harissa condiment Yield: 3 (2/3 cup) servings

1 ½ cups pimiento, drained
1 tablespoon fresh garlic, chopped
1 ½ tablespoons olive oil
1 teaspoon caraway seeds, toasted

½ teaspoon ground cayenne pepper
½ teaspoon ground coriander
¼ teaspoon ground cumin

INSTRUCTIONS:

Follow the prep technique next to each ingredient.

In a food processor purée the harissa condiment and set aside.

In a small pot bring the water to a boil. Add quinoa, bring it back to a boil, cover and reduce heat to a low simmer. Cook until water is evaporated. Remove from heat and fluff. Set aside. While quinoa is cooking, heat olive oil in a skillet and sauté peppers followed by the eggplant, adding the yellow and zucchini squash. Add small amounts of water to prevent the vegetables from burning. Add spices and desired amount of the harissa. Keep sautéing to extract their aroma, fold in the tomatoes and add the necessary amount of water to prevent them from sticking. Fold in the cooked quinoa, mix well and serve.

CATEGORY TAGS:

- ◉ gluten-free
- ○ high fiber
- ○ high protein
- ○ low calorie
- ◉ low carbohydrate / low sugar
- ◉ low cholesterol
- ○ low fat / low saturated fat
- ◉ low sodium
- ◉ vegan
- ◉ vegetarian
- ◉ whole food plant based
- ◉ whole grain

NUTRITIONAL DATA:

calories	143.24
fat	4.64g
sat fat	0.64g
cholesterol	0mg
sodium	121.68mg
carbohydrates	21.72g
fiber	2.57g
sugars	1.79g
protein	4.66g

Golden Roast Fennel Mashed Potatoes

The very thought of combining sweet, golden potatoes and the slightly anise, slightly sweet taste of roasted fennel should be enough to make any mouth water. Certainly not the boring mash we've grown accustomed to, this side is easy enough to become a regular favorite, with abundant flavor to sit alongside a special roast or spicy dish. Fennel provides nutrients helpful in digestion and is rich in iron and potassium. It softens in the oven, giving up some of its licorice quality as it sweetens, and gives a mellow richness to the versatile Yukon.

PREP INSTRUCTIONS:

Yield: 20 (1/2 cup) servings
Prep Time: 20 minutes

Cooking Time: 45 minutes
Total Time: 1 hour 5 minutes

RECIPE INGREDIENTS:

3 lbs. golden potatoes, peeled and diced
2 cups yellow onions, sliced
2 ¼ lbs. fennel, sliced
3 tablespoons olive oil
1 teaspoon kosher salt

INSTRUCTIONS:

Follow the prep technique next to each ingredient.

Pre-heat oven to 375°F.

Combine fennel and onions with half the oil and place in an oven proof pan, cover with foil and bake at 375 degrees for 45 minutes. Remove from the oven and puree in a food processor until smooth. Steam or boil the potatoes. Remove from the steamer or drain. In a mixer mash the potatoes folding in the fennel puree with the remaining olive oil and the seasonings. Do not over beat. Serve hot.

CATEGORY TAGS:

- ◉ gluten-free
- ◉ high fiber
- ○ high protein
- ○ low calorie
- ◉ low carbohydrate / low sugar
- ◉ low cholesterol
- ◉ low fat / low saturated fat
- ○ low sodium
- ◉ vegan
- ◉ vegetarian
- ◉ whole food plant based
- ○ whole grain

NUTRITIONAL DATA:

calories	90.21
fat	2.22g
sat fat	0.34g
cholesterol	0mg
sodium	144.92mg
carbohydrates	17.70g
fiber	3.10g
sugars	2.69g
protein	2.07g

Thyme and Date Stuffing

You might think of "stuffing" as something that needs a large turkey and a massive family gathering to enjoy. Not so! In fact, a stuffing cooked outside a bird is called dressing, and a delightful dress this is. The combination of sweet apricots and dates, deeply savory garlic, and onions and crunchy and silky textures of breads and nuts will keep even the most distractible guest interested. Preparation is easy—get someone to help chop—and the aroma of fresh herbs will attract attention before the first bite.

PREP INSTRUCTIONS:

Yield: 18 (1/2 cup) servings
Prep Time: 10 minutes

Cooking Time: 30 minutes
Total Time: 40 minutes

RECIPE INGREDIENTS:

¼ cup olive oil
2 ½ cups celery, diced
2 ½ cups yellow onion, diced
4 cups mushrooms, sliced
2 teaspoons fresh garlic, minced
1 tablespoon dried apricot, chopped
2 tablespoons dates, chopped
2 tablespoons walnuts, toasted and chopped

1 ½ tablespoons fresh sage, chopped
1 ½ tablespoons fresh thyme, chopped
1/16 teaspoon ground nutmeg
1/16 teaspoon ground cloves
½ teaspoon ground black pepper
1 to 1 ½ cups low sodium chicken broth
18 oz. whole wheat bread cut into cubes
Nonstick cooking spray

INSTRUCTIONS:

Follow the prep technique next to each ingredient.

Preheat oven to 350˚F

In a medium saucepan combine olive oil, celery, onions, mushrooms, garlic, fresh herbs and broth. Cover and sauté on medium heat just until soft. Combine bread, dried fruit, walnuts and spices with the wet ingredients. Spray a casserole with nonstick cooking spray and add the stuffing mixture. Bake covered for 20 minutes. Uncover and bake 10 more minutes for a crisp crust.

CATEGORY TAGS:

- ○ gluten-free
- ◉ high fiber
- ○ high protein
- ○ low calorie
- ◉ low carbohydrate / low sugar
- ◉ low cholesterol
- ○ low fat / low saturated fat
- ◉ low sodium
- ◉ vegan
- ◉ vegetarian
- ◉ whole food plant based
- ◉ whole grain

NUTRITIONAL DATA:

calories	135
fat	5g
sat fat	0.54g
cholesterol	0.25mg
sodium	127mg
carbohydrates	17g
fiber	3.34g
sugars	4.30g
protein	5g

Sweet Potato, Sweet Parsnip Mash

Unlike its relative, the carrot, parsnips benefit from a long, slow cook to release their inherent sweetness. Joined with sweet potatoes, they become a fragrant side dish that is hard to turn down, while supplying some important health benefits: both vegetables are high in vitamins with good levels of potassium and complex carbohydrates. But it's the taste that matters, and this simple combination delivers.

PREP INSTRUCTIONS:

Yield: 10 (1/2 cup) servings
Prep Time: 5 minutes

Cooking Time: 25 minutes
Total Time: 30 minutes

RECIPE INGREDIENTS:

2 lbs. sweet potato, peeled and cut into chunks
1 ½ cups parsnips, peeled and diced
¼ cup nonfat Greek yogurt
¼ teaspoon kosher salt
½ teaspoon ground white pepper
pinch of nutmeg
1 tablespoon parsley, chopped

INSTRUCTIONS:

Follow the prep technique next to each ingredient.

Place potatoes and parsnips in a steam basket. Cover and cook until tender, about 20 to 25 minutes. Transfer to a mixer, incorporate the rest of the ingredients and mash until soft.

CATEGORY TAGS:

- ◉ gluten-free
- ◉ high fiber
- ○ high protein
- ○ low calorie
- ◉ low carbohydrate / low sugar
- ◉ low cholesterol
- ◉ low fat / low saturated fat
- ◉ low sodium
- ○ vegan
- ◉ vegetarian
- ○ whole food plant based
- ○ whole grain

NUTRITIONAL DATA:

calories	96.92
fat	0.12g
sat fat	0.03g
cholesterol	0mg
sodium	102.78mg
carbohydrates	22.19g
fiber	3.73g
sugars	4.99g
protein	2.29g

Italian Mushroom Seasoned Polenta

Polenta, and cakes made from it, are dishes enjoyed in Italy for centuries—not bad, considering they didn't have corn until it arrived from the New World in the 1500s. But grains slow simmered into a porridge are a hearty and flavorful dish, especially when combined with mushrooms and a dash of red pepper for spice. The combination of polenta and mushrooms in particular is potent, boosting each other's antioxidant health benefits. Try this recipe using coarse, stone-ground grits and lemon thyme with a bit of freshly-grated lemon zest for a bright, toothy variation.

PREP INSTRUCTIONS:

Yield: 8 (1/2 cup) servings
Prep Time: 5 minutes

Cooking Time: 7 minutes
Total Time: 12 minutes

RECIPE INGREDIENTS:

1 ½ teaspoons olive oil
1 cup mushrooms, sliced
¾ teaspoon fresh thyme, minced
¾ teaspoon fresh garlic, minced
¾ cup polenta, dry

2 ¼ cups water
2 tablespoons fresh parsley, chopped
A pinch of nutmeg
¼ teaspoon red pepper flakes

INSTRUCTIONS:

Follow the prep technique next to each ingredient.

In a medium size skillet sauté mushrooms, using water to avoid burning. After mushrooms are cooked, add thyme and garlic; cook until the aroma is released. Set aside. In a medium saucepan, bring the water to a boil and slowly add the polenta, stirring continuously as it starts to thicken. Add the seasoning and fold in the mushroom mixture. Remove from heat and serve or place into a shallow dish and refrigerate for later use. After complete cool down you can shape it as desired, sear it, or grill it.

CATEGORY TAGS:

- ◉ gluten-free
- ○ high fiber
- ○ high protein
- ○ low calorie
- ◉ low carbohydrate / low sugar
- ◉ low cholesterol
- ◉ low fat / low saturated fat
- ◉ low sodium
- ◉ vegan
- ◉ vegetarian
- ◉ whole food plant based
- ○ whole grain

NUTRITIONAL DATA:

calories	71.16
fat	0.93g
sat fat	0.13g
cholesterol	0mg
sodium	33.11mg
carbohydrates	14.13g
fiber	1.66g
sugars	0.19g
protein	1.85g

Herb-scented Quinoa with Swiss Chard

Hard to believe that the sagebrush, known as tumbleweed from all those old cowboy movies, is a relative of the now highly-regarded quinoa plant, found in the high Andes mountains for thousands of years. These chewy seeds are called one of the "superfoods", a gluten-free marvel with lots of protein, fiber and calcium. But the fluffy texture and depth of taste will make anyone forget it's good for them, and this savory combination of flavors, highlighted by fresh herbs, raisins and almost sweet chard, is a great way to serve a healthy meal. Soaking the raisins before hitting the sauté pan will bring out even more flavor.

PREP INSTRUCTIONS:

Yield: 20 (3/4 cup) servings
Prep Time: 15 minutes

Cooking Time: 15 minutes
Total Time: 30 minutes

RECIPE INGREDIENTS:

2 cups quinoa, dry
3 ½ cups water
2 teaspoons olive oil
⅔ cup shallots, chopped
3 cups mushrooms, sliced
1 tablespoon garlic, minced
2 teaspoons rosemary, chopped
1 teaspoon fresh thyme, minced

¾ cup carrot, shredded
1 teaspoon kosher salt
¼ teaspoon crushed red pepper
3 plum tomatoes, chopped
½ cup golden raisins
2 tablespoons lemon juice
4 cups Swiss chard, shredded and steamed

INSTRUCTIONS:

Follow the prep technique next to each ingredient.

In a small saucepan combine quinoa and water and bring to a boil. Cover and lower the heat to medium low (simmer). Cook until water is absorbed, 15 to 20 minutes. Meanwhile sauté shallots and mushrooms in olive oil until they release most of their liquid; add the garlic, fresh herbs and carrots. Season with salt and crushed red pepper. Add the tomatoes, lemon juice and golden raisins. Fold in the steamed Swiss chard and bring to temperature. Combine quinoa with the Swiss chard-tomato mixture and serve warm.

CATEGORY TAGS:

- ◉ gluten-free
- ○ high fiber
- ○ high protein
- ○ low calorie
- ◉ low carbohydrate / low sugar
- ◉ low cholesterol
- ◉ low fat / low saturated fat
- ◉ low sodium
- ◉ vegan
- ◉ vegetarian
- ◉ whole food plant based
- ◉ whole grain

NUTRITIONAL DATA:

calories	98.86
fat	1.58g
sat fat	0.09g
cholesterol	0mg
sodium	169.38mg
carbohydrates	18.46g
fiber	2.29g
sugars	4.42g
protein	3.78g

Fresh Lemon Basil and Tomato Bruschetta

The Italian table loves bruschetta, a Roman way of using leftover bread to bring the freshest tomatoes and local olive oil to a meal. Properly pronounced with a hard "k" (brusketta), Roman cooks will usually toast the bread and then rub raw garlic cloves over its sandpapery surface to spread the flavor, but this finely-minced addition ensures that the great health benefits of fresh garlic are used to their best advantage. In fact, just about every ingredient of this dish makes good heart sense. A small bottle of good olive oil is a great investment to the taste and nutrition of this dish.

PREP INSTRUCTIONS:

Yield: 16 (2 slices each) servings
Prep Time: 10 minutes

Cooking Time: 5 minutes
Total Time: 15 minutes

RECIPE INGREDIENTS:

32 slices of whole wheat French loaf
12 oz. plum tomatoes, diced
1 teaspoon fresh garlic, minced
¼ cup red onions, diced
¼ sundried tomatoes, minced
1 ½ tablespoons olive oil
1 tablespoon lemon juice
3 tablespoons parmesan cheese, grated
¼ cup Italian parsley, chopped
1 tablespoon fresh basil, chopped

INSTRUCTIONS:

Follow the prep technique next to each ingredient.

Pre-heat oven to 350°F

Place bread on a sheet pan and toast for 5 minutes. Remove from oven and let cool completely. Combine all the ingredients for the bruschetta. Place two tablespoons of the tomato mixture on each toast and serve.

CATEGORY TAGS:

○ gluten-free
○ high fiber
○ high protein
○ low calorie
◉ low carbohydrate / low sugar
◉ low cholesterol
◉ low fat / low saturated fat
◉ low sodium
○ vegan
◉ vegetarian
○ whole food plant based
◉ whole grain

NUTRITIONAL DATA:

calories	71.09
fat	2.41g
sat fat	0.37g
cholesterol	0mg
sodium	99.75mg
carbohydrates	10.51g
fiber	1.98g
sugars	1.97g
protein	3.81g

Quinoa and Roasted Squash with Peppers

The ancient grain called quinoa has a history that stretches back 3,000 years to South America, yet still elicits quizzical looks and odd pronunciations (it's KEEN-wa). This relative of beets and spinach, high in protein and gluten-free, has a nutty, creamy consistency and makes for a great base for slow-roasted vegetables with their own smoky, rich flavors. This dish is a fine side dish for chicken or fish, or as a meat-free main course.

PREP INSTRUCTIONS:

Yield: 10 (1/2 cup) servings
Prep Time: 10 minutes

Cooking Time: 30 minutes
Total Time: 40 minutes

RECIPE INGREDIENTS:

1 cup quinoa, dry
1 ¾ cups water
⅓ cup yellow squash, chopped
⅓ cup zucchini squash, chopped
½ teaspoon kosher salt
¾ teaspoon ground black pepper
2 cups butternut squash, chopped
dash of nutmeg

1 tablespoon olive oil
½ cup red bell pepper, chopped
½ cup plum tomato, chopped
½ teaspoon paprika
½ cup scallions, cut into ¼ inch bias cut
¼ cup Italian parsley, chopped
2 tablespoons lemon juice
Non-stick cooking spray

INSTRUCTIONS:

Follow the prep technique next to each ingredient. Preheat oven to 350˚F. In a medium sauce pan with a lid place water and bring to a boil. Add the quinoa and bring it back to a boil. Cover and lower heat to low. Simmer for 15-20 minutes. Fluff quinoa and set aside.

Meanwhile season the yellow and zucchini squash with salt and pepper, spray nonstick cooking spray on the vegetables and place on prepared sheet pan. Season the butternut squash with nutmeg and place on prepared sheet pan. Roast vegetables in the oven for approximately 12-15 minutes. The butternut squash may take around 20 - 25 minutes depending on the oven.

In a skillet sauté the red peppers, tomatoes and Scallions in olive oil until fragrant, add lemon juice and paprika. Combine cooked quinoa with all the vegetables, fold in the parsley and serve.

CATEGORY TAGS:

◉ gluten-free
○ high fiber
○ high protein
○ low calorie
◉ low carbohydrate / low sugar
◉ low cholesterol
◉ low fat / low saturated fat
◉ low sodium
◉ vegan
◉ vegetarian
◉ whole food plant based
◉ whole grain

NUTRITIONAL DATA:

calories	98.54
fat	2.47g
sat fat	0.21g
cholesterol	0mg
sodium1	45.16mg
carbohydrates	16.94g
fiber	1.90g
sugars	1.70g
protein	3.12g

Kale, Farro and Griddled Mushrooms

There is such depth of flavor in this combination of greens, grains and mushrooms that the nutritional value is almost secondary--but it's not. Kale is an amazing high protein source of vitamins A, K and C (1,000% more than cooked spinach), minerals like copper, potassium and iron, and has become so popular, it should have its own television show. Barely cooked, the deep green leaves make a healthy backdrop for the nutty whole grain farro, an ancient European form of wheat with a chewy texture and hints of cinnamon flavor. The antioxidant benefits of cabbage, vitamin-rich mushrooms, and the fiber and protein of farro all in one dish.

PREP INSTRUCTIONS:

Yield: 10 (1/2 cup) servings
Prep Time: 10 minutes

Cooking Time: 40 minutes
Total Time: 50 minutes

RECIPE INGREDIENTS:

1 cup whole grain farro, dry
2 cups water
4 cups kale, stems removed,
    cut into bite size and steamed
1 tablespoon olive oil
2 cups cremini mushrooms, sliced
⅓ cup shallots, chopped
2-3 cloves garlic, minced

1 tablespoon rosemary
¼ cup sundried tomatoes, chopped
⅛ teaspoon ground black pepper
Pinch of nutmeg
¾ cup low sodium chicken broth
2 tablespoons lemon juice
¼ cup fresh basil, shredded
1 ½ teaspoon parmesan cheese, grated

INSTRUCTIONS:

Follow the prep technique next to each ingredient.

Place farro with water in a medium pot, bring to a boil, cover with a lid and simmer for 30 to 40 minutes or until farro is tender. Drain and set aside. Steam kale, and shock in cold water to keep its color. Set aside.

In a sauté pan add olive oil, sauté the mushrooms, add shallots, garlic, sundried tomatoes and rosemary. Carefully pour the chicken broth, pepper and nutmeg; reduce to almost dried. Then add the lemon juice, the cooked farro, steamed kale and fresh basil.

Serve with parmesan cheese on the side.

CATEGORY TAGS:

O gluten-free
O high fiber
O high protein
O low calorie
◉ low carbohydrate / low sugar
◉ low cholesterol
◉ low fat / low saturated fat
◉ low sodium
O vegan
O vegetarian
O whole food plant based
◉ whole grain

NUTRITIONAL DATA:

calories	99.95
fat	1.62g
sat fat	0.30g
cholesterol	0.59g
sodium	43.04mg
carbohydrates	18.26g
fiber	2.33g
sugars	1.67g
protein	4.46g

ENTRÉES

Spaghetti Squash with Marinara Sauce

The best lesson to learn from this recipe is that homemade sauce is easier and tastier than you think. The antioxidant benefits of tomatoes are well documented, and the taste of simmered crushed tomatoes infuses into the entire dish. Spaghetti squash is gluten-free and high in folic acid, vitamin A and potassium, a great reason for the health-conscious to skip pasta and go for this tasty alternative.

PREP INSTRUCTIONS:

Yield: 8 (1/2 cup) servings
Prep Time: 20 minutes

Cooking Time: 40 minutes
Total Time: 1 hour and five minutes

RECIPE INGREDIENTS:

3 lbs. spaghetti squash, as purchased

For the Marinara sauce

1 tablespoon olive oil
1 ½ cups yellow onion, diced
3 tablespoons garlic, chopped
1 ½ teaspoons dried basil
2 teaspoons dried oregano
1 tablespoon fresh thyme, chopped

⅛ teaspoon chili flakes
6 cups diced tomatoes in juice
2 cups crushed tomatoes
½ teaspoon kosher salt
¾ teaspoon honey
½ cup fresh basil

INSTRUCTIONS:

Follow the prep technique for each ingredient. Preheat oven to 350°F.

Cut spaghetti squash in half lengthwise; remove the seeds. In a roasting pan place the squash open face down. Add water to cover at least 1/8 of the squash. Bake squash 45 minutes and scrape the spaghetti strands. While the squash is roasting, place the olive oil in a medium saucepan and sauté the onions, garlic, herbs and spices.

When onions start to get translucent add the rest of the ingredients except the fresh basil. Simmer sauce 20 to 25 minutes. Remove from heat, add fresh basil and purée sauce in a blender. Return sauce back to heat source and simmer 5 more minutes.

Divide the spaghetti squash into servings and serve with 3 oz. marinara sauce.

CATEGORY TAGS:

- ◉ gluten-free
- ○ high fiber
- ○ high protein
- ○ low calorie
- ◉ low carbohydrate / low sugar
- ◉ low cholesterol
- ◉ low fat / low saturated fat
- ○ low sodium
- ◉ vegan
- ◉ vegetarian
- ◉ whole food plant based
- ○ whole grain

NUTRITIONAL DATA:

calories	35.27
fat	0.66g
sat fat	0.10g
cholesterol	0mg
sodium	251.60mg
carbohydrates	6.15g
fiber	1.69g
sugars	2.35g
protein	1.12g

Salmon with Tomato and Mango Salsa

A bright and taste-tempting meal any time of the year, but particularly when mangoes are available fresh from the grocer. Loaded with antioxidants, natural fiber and a healthy boost of vitamins C and A, mangoes add great value along with a unique taste, matching surprisingly well with tomatoes and basil. Look for wild-caught West Coast salmon for the best quality, high nutrition omega-3 essential fatty acids, a great supplement to the health of your heart.

PREP INSTRUCTIONS:

Yield: 8 servings
Prep Time: 10 minutes

Cooking Time: 15 minutes
Total Time: 25 minutes

RECIPE INGREDIENTS:

For the Salsa:

1 cup fresh mango, chopped
2 plum tomatoes, chopped
4 tablespoons red onion, diced
2 teaspoon fresh garlic, minced
2 teaspoons fresh thyme, minced
2 teaspoons fresh tarragon, chopped

2 tablespoons fresh basil, chopped
2 tablespoons golden balsamic vinegar
½ teaspoon olive oil
⅛ teaspoon black pepper
⅛ teaspoon kosher salt

For the Salmon

8-3 to 4 oz. salmon fillets
1 teaspoon garlic powder
2 teaspoons fresh oregano, minced

¼ teaspoon ground black pepper
2 teaspoons fresh thyme, minced

INSTRUCTIONS:

Follow the prep technique next to each ingredient. Preheat oven to 325˚F. Prepare pan with nonstick cooking spray. Dice tomatoes, mango and onions to make the salsa. Add the vinegar, olive oil, fresh tarragon, garlic, kosher salt and black pepper. Set aside.

Season the salmon fillets with the rest of the ingredients. Place fish on a prepared sheet pan and bake 12-15 minutes. Serve with Tomato and Mango Salsa.

CATEGORY TAGS:

- ◉ gluten-free
- ○ high fiber
- ○ high protein
- ○ low calorie
- ◉ low carbohydrate / low sugar
- ◉ low cholesterol
- ○ low fat / low saturated fat
- ◉ low sodium
- ○ vegan
- ○ vegetarian
- ○ whole food plant based
- ○ whole grain

NUTRITIONAL DATA:

calories	143.07
fat	5.16g
sat fat	0.84g
cholesterol	49.33mg
sodium	81.95mg
carbohydrates	5.16g
fiber	0.70g
sugars	3.40g
protein	19.67g

Asian Garlic and Ginger Chicken

The combination of fresh garlic and ginger has been a healthful, flavorful addition to Thai and Indian cuisine for centuries, and adds an Asian note to this simple preparation of low fat chicken breast. The ginger and garlic flavors add a level of spice and sweet/savory notes, and the entire dish makes for a beneficial chicken soup alternative; both garlic and ginger are uncommon answers to warding off and alleviating the common cold.

PREP INSTRUCTIONS:

Yield: 4 servings
Prep Time: 5 minutes

Cooking Time: 20 minutes
Total Time: 25 minutes

RECIPE INGREDIENTS:

4 (4 oz.) chicken breast
1 tablespoon sesame seeds, toasted
1 tablespoon fresh ginger, minced
½ tablespoon fresh garlic, minced
1 teaspoon low sodium soy sauce
1 tablespoon scallions, thinly sliced
1 tablespoon sweet chili sauce

INSTRUCTIONS:

Follow the prep technique next to each ingredient.

Preheat oven to 350°F. Prepare pan with nonstick cooking spray.

Marinate chicken with all the ingredients except the sesame seeds for at least 2 hours prior to cooking. Place on a prepared sheet pan, sprinkle the sesame seeds and bake for 15-20 minutes or until internal temperature reaches 165 F.

CATEGORY TAGS:

- ◉ gluten-free
- ○ high fiber
- ○ high protein
- ○ low calorie
- ◉ low carbohydrate / low sugar
- ◉ low cholesterol
- ○ low fat / low saturated fat
- ◉ low sodium
- ○ vegan
- ○ vegetarian
- ○ whole food plant based
- ○ whole grain

NUTRITIONAL DATA:

calories	184.12
fat	5.71g
sat fat	1.51g
cholesterol	75.00mg
sodium	112.94mg
carbohydrates	2.96g
fiber	0.36g
sugars	1.70g
protein	29.30g

Sage, Rosemary and Thyme Turkey Breast

It's a shame that turkey gets overlooked unless it is a holiday, but fork-for-fork, this noble bird (Benjamin Franklin wanted the turkey, not the eagle, as America's national symbol) has more taste and texture than your average chicken. Fresh sage, rosemary and thyme add fragrance and earthy tastes to the roasted breast (try experimenting with different thyme flavors such as lemon or mint—there are dozens of varieties), and you'll marvel at the added flavor that comes from the addition (and removal) of the turkey skin during cooking.

PREP INSTRUCTIONS:

Yield: 18 (4 oz) servings
Prep Time: 15 minutes

Cooking Time: 45 minutes
Total Time: 60 minutes

RECIPE INGREDIENTS:

5 lb. turkey breast with skin on
1 teaspoon olive oil
1 teaspoon lemon zest
¼ cup lemon juice
1 tablespoon fresh garlic, minced

1 tablespoon fresh thyme, chopped
2 tablespoons fresh sage, chopped
2 tablespoons fresh rosemary, chopped
1 teaspoon kosher salt
¼ teaspoon ground black pepper

INSTRUCTIONS:

Follow the prep technique next to each ingredient.

Preheat oven to 325 ˚F.

Remove the skin from the turkey (do not discard). Combine the rest of the ingredients to make a rub.

Rub turkey breast with the fresh herb rub and cover it back with the skin. Place turkey on a roasting rack and roast for about 1 hour or until its temperature reaches 165 degrees. Let it stand 5 to 10 minutes; remove the skin (discard skin to lower the fat consumption). Slice and serve.

CATEGORY TAGS:

- ◉ gluten-free
- ○ high fiber
- ○ high protein
- ○ low calorie
- ◉ low carbohydrate / low sugar
- ◉ low cholesterol
- ◉ low fat / low saturated fat
- ○ low sodium
- ○ vegan
- ○ vegetarian
- ○ whole food plant based
- ○ whole grain

NUTRITIONAL DATA:

calories	150.05
fat	2.09g
sat fat	0.62g
cholesterol	66.67mg
sodium	217.98mg
carbohydrates	1.65g
fiber	0.01g
sugars	0.09g
protein	26.74g

Container Garden Spring Chicken

This colorful and flavorful dish would make good use of a container gardener's best: peppers, rosemary and parsley. The long marinade in oil and lemon will give a tender appeal to the chicken, and the flavors of fresh garlic, spicy chili and sweet paprika make for a pepper trifecta that brings a Continental flair to the meal. Serve with rice to savor every bit of the marinade, or dice leftovers for an interesting twist on chicken salad.

PREP INSTRUCTIONS:

Yield: 8 servings
Prep Time: 10 minutes

Cooking Time: 20-25 minutes
Total Time: 35 minutes

RECIPE INGREDIENTS:

8 (4 oz) chicken breasts
1 tablespoon olive oil
¾ cup red bell pepper, chopped
1 teaspoon garlic, minced
1 ½ teaspoons fresh thyme, minced
1 tablespoon Italian parsley, chopped

1 ½ teaspoons lemon zest
¼ cup lemon juice
¼ teaspoon red crushed pepper
1 teaspoon ground black pepper
¾ teaspoon paprika
¼ teaspoon kosher salt

INSTRUCTIONS:

Follow the prep technique next to each ingredient.

Preheat oven to 350°F. Prepare pan with nonstick spray.

To make marinade, combine all ingredients in a food processor except the chicken and pulse to mince or to a chunky consistency. Marinate the chicken at least 3 hours before cooking. Place chicken on a prepared sheet pan using all the marinade. Bake for 20-25 minutes or until internal temperature reaches 165 degrees.

CATEGORY TAGS:

- ◉ gluten-free
- ○ high fiber
- ○ high protein
- ○ low calorie
- ◉ low carbohydrate / low sugar
- ○ low cholesterol
- ○ low fat / low saturated fat
- ◉ low sodium
- ○ vegan
- ○ vegetarian
- ○ whole food plant based
- ○ whole grain

NUTRITIONAL DATA:

calories	144.98
fat	3.91g
sat fat	1.29g
cholesterol	75.94mg
sodium	137.99mg
carbohydrates	1.82g
fiber	0.70g
sugars	0.62g
protein	26.67g

Sesame Baked Asian Tofu

The complex whole proteins provided by tofu are an easy way to balance a diet that may go astray now and then. This recipe has a great combination of silky tofu, the airy, large flake crunch of Japanese panko breadcrumbs, and the nutty toothiness of sesame seeds. Tofu is a blank slate for flavors, soaking up the Asian influences of rice vinegar, the sweet heat of chili sauce and honey, and the unmistakable savory taste of sesame oil. A citrus-accented salad or sautéed spinach will make this dish a complete meal.

PREP INSTRUCTIONS:

Yield: 8 servings
Prep Time: 10 minutes

Cooking Time: 15 minutes
Total Time: 25 minutes

RECIPE INGREDIENTS:

1 block of extra firm tofu, drained and pressed
1 ½ teaspoons sesame oil
2 tablespoons rice vinegar
1 tablespoon sweet chili sauce
4 tablespoons honey
1 teaspoon granulated garlic
2 ½ tablespoons sesame seeds, toasted
¾ cup whole-wheat Panko bread crumbs

INSTRUCTIONS:

Measure the ingredients.

Preheat the oven at 375° F.

Cut tofu into 8 pieces. Combine the whole-wheat panko and sesame seeds in a pan. Whisk together the sesame oil, rice vinegar, sweet chili sauce, honey and granulated garlic to make a brine. Baste each tofu steak in the brine, then coat each steak with the sesame-panko mixture. Place on a baking sheet with parchment paper and bake until golden brown, about 15 minutes. Serve hot.

CATEGORY TAGS:

○ gluten-free
○ high fiber
○ high protein
○ low calorie
◉ low carbohydrate / low sugar
◉ low cholesterol
○ low fat / low saturated fat
◉ low sodium
○ vegan
◉ vegetarian
◉ whole food plant based
○ whole grain

NUTRITIONAL DATA:

calories	127.14
fat	5.06g
sat fat	0.44g
cholesterol	0mg
sodium	23.16mg
carbohydrates	14.20g
fiber	1.26g
sugars	6.28g
protein	6.33g

Middle Eastern Falafel Patties

The joys of the chickpea are known world wide, from Bronze Age Greece to ancient Rome. Garbanzos are used to make fritters in Israel and France, fried and spiced as curry in India, soaked in syrup in the Philippines and even ground and brewed like coffee in Germany. This dish celebrates the nutty taste and versatility of the chickpea by adding Middle Eastern flavors for a hearty vegetarian meal. Stuff it into a pita bread with tomato, lettuce and parsley for an authentic delight.

PREP INSTRUCTIONS:

Yield: 14 (3 oz) servings
Prep Time: 10 minutes

Cooking Time: 25 minutes
Total Time: 35 minutes

RECIPE INGREDIENTS:

14 oz. garbanzo beans, dry
8 cups water, for soaking
1 ½ cups yellow onion, diced
2 tablespoons fresh garlic, chopped
1 tablespoon ground cumin
1 tablespoon paprika
2 teaspoons coriander
¼ teaspoon ground cayenne pepper

½ teaspoon baking soda
1 teaspoon kosher salt
4 tablespoons all-purpose flour
4 tablespoons sesame, toasted
¼ cup Italian parsley, chopped
¼ cup cilantro, chopped
1 tablespoon lemon juice
2 tablespoons olive oil

INSTRUCTIONS:

Follow the prep technique for each ingredient. Preheat oven to 375°F.

In a large bowl place garbanzos and cover with water at least 3 times its volume. Let them soak overnight or until you can break them apart with your fingers, drain and set aside.

Place all ingredients into a food processor and pulse until it acquires a minced consistency, do not purée. Shape into 3oz patties. Brush both sides with olive oil and place on a prepared sheet pan with parchment paper and bake 15 to 20 minutes.

Optional, pan sear in olive oil before baking (this procedure will add more fat to the finished product) to golden brown, before placing in the oven.

CATEGORY TAGS:

O gluten-free
● high fiber
O high protein
O low calorie
● low carbohydrate / low sugar
● low cholesterol
O low fat / low saturated fat
O low sodium
● vegan
● vegetarian
● whole food plant based
O whole grain

NUTRITIONAL DATA:

calories	156.30
fat	5.13g
sat fat	0.30g
cholesterol	0mg
sodium	196.62mg
carbohydrates	21.55g
fiber	6.10g
sugars	4.00g
protein	7.02g

Crispy Pumpkin Seed Chicken

You might not think of pumpkin seeds as chicken coating material, but these nutty, chewy kernels are every bit as tasty and versatile as almonds or pistachios in cooking. One of the most popular snacks in the world, pumpkin seeds (called pepitas in Mexico) add texture and a unique taste, and are one of the best sources of magnesium, zinc and amino acids available. This recipe has many levels of flavor, from a complex mix of sweet and tart via honey and balsamic, a Spanish flair of thyme, peppers and cumin, and the toasty appeal of pepitas.

PREP INSTRUCTIONS:

Yield: 6 (4 oz) servings
Prep Time: 10 minutes

Cooking Time: 15 minutes
Total Time: 25 minutes

RECIPE INGREDIENTS:

6 (4 oz) chicken breast
1 cup whole-wheat Panko bread crumbs
½ cup pumpkin seeds, toasted
1 ½ tablespoons fresh thyme, minced
¼ cup fresh parsley
¾ teaspoon paprika

¾ teaspoon granulated garlic
½ teaspoon ground chipotle
1 teaspoon ground cumin
¾ teaspoon kosher salt
¼ cup balsamic vinegar
¼ cup honey

INSTRUCTIONS:

Follow the prep technique next to each ingredient.

Preheat oven to 350°F.

Combine all dried ingredients together to make the breadcrumbs mixture.

For basting: combine vinegar and honey. Pat dry chicken breasts and baste with balsamic mixture and coat with pumpkin breading (making sure to keep pumpkin mixture dry). Place chicken on a baking sheet with parchment paper and bake 15 to 20 minutes or until internal temperature reaches 165 degrees.

CATEGORY TAGS:

O gluten-free
O high fiber
O high protein
O low calorie
◉ low carbohydrate / low sugar
O low cholesterol
O low fat / low saturated fat
O low sodium
O vegan
O vegetarian
O whole food plant based
O whole grain

NUTRITIONAL DATA:

calories	0
fat	6.80g
sat fat	1.69g
cholesterol	75.94mg
sodium	337.62mg
carbohydrates	12.62g
fiber	1.73g
sugars	2.55g
protein	30.95g

Creamy Mascarpone Polenta with Squash Ribbon Spaghetti

Ciao, bella! This molto Italiano dish turns pasta on its head by putting the actual pasta below the "noodles." Made of thin ribbons of yellow and green squash, mingled with that strangest of gourds—the spaghetti—and supported by a creamy and indulgent mascarpone polenta. Think cheese grits, Neapolitan style.

PREP INSTRUCTIONS:

Yield: 8 servings
Prep Time: 20 minutes

Cooking Time: 50 minutes
Total Time: 1 hour, 10 minutes

RECIPE INGREDIENTS:

For the Three-squash Spaghetti:
4 cups spaghetti squash, cooked (about 3 lbs. whole)
1 ½ cups zucchini squash, seeded and thinly sliced
1 ½ cups yellow squash, seeded and thinly sliced
¾ cup carrots, julienned
¾ cup plum tomatoes, seeded and diced
½ teaspoon olive oil

2 teaspoons fresh garlic, minced
1 tablespoon fresh basil, shredded
½ teaspoon fine black pepper
1 teaspoon Italian parsley, chopped
a pinch of kosher salt

For the Mascarpone Polenta:
1 ½ cups skim milk
½ cup water
1 cup polenta
a pinch of nutmeg

½ teaspoon marjoram
½ teaspoon rubbed sage
⅛ teaspoon cayenne pepper
3 tablespoons mascarpone cheese

INSTRUCTIONS:

Follow the prep technique next to each ingredient. Preheat oven to 350˚ F.

Cut spaghetti squash lengthwise; remove seeds. Place squash face down in a roasting pan; add water to cover at least ¼ inch of the squash. Place in the oven; cook for 35-45 minutes. Remove from oven and scrape the inside. Set aside. In a heated skillet, add the olive oil; sauté the zucchini, yellow squash and carrots, adding water to create steam. Add the diced tomatoes and garlic. Fold in the spaghetti squash, fresh herbs and spices.

For the Mascarpone polenta:

Place the liquid ingredients and spices in a small saucepan; simmer over medium heat. Slowly drizzle polenta; whisk constantly until it thickens. Add the mascarpone cheese; mix well. Serve mascarpone polenta with three-squash spaghetti.

CATEGORY TAGS:

- ◉ gluten-free
- ◉ high fiber
- ○ high protein
- ○ low calorie
- ◉ low carbohydrate / low sugar
- ◉ low cholesterol
- ○ low fat / low saturated fat
- ○ low sodium
- ○ vegan
- ◉ vegetarian
- ○ whole food plant based
- ○ whole grain

NUTRITIONAL DATA:

calories	202.96
fat	7.65g
sat fat	3.27
cholesterol	12.70mg
sodium	218.99mg
carbohydrates	20.75g
fiber	3.33g
sugars	11.39g
protein	5.62g

Portobello Chard Sauté with Whole Wheat Pasta

Highly nutritious and much prized, Swiss chard is not only tasty but surprisingly beautiful, whether dark green or wearing stalks of many colors as the rainbow variety. It's also not from Switzerland at all, but keep its secret and enjoy. The flavor of the chard, halfway between spinach and collards, sets off against the nutty whole wheat pasta and meaty mushrooms nicely, and the sautéed stalks add extra dash of fiber and flavor.

PREP INSTRUCTIONS:

Yield: 8 (3/4 cup) servings
Prep Time: 10 minutes

Cooking Time: 10 minutes
Total Time: 20 minutes

RECIPE INGREDIENTS:

8 oz. whole wheat angel hair pasta
1 ½ tablespoons olive oil
½ cup Swiss chard stalks, thinly sliced
1 ½ cups portobello mushrooms, clean and sliced
½ cup shallots, thinly sliced
1 tablespoon fresh garlic, minced

¼ cup vegetable broth
⅛ teaspoon crushed red pepper
1 teaspoon kosher salt
6 cups or ½ lb. Swiss chard, shredded
Fresh ground black pepper

INSTRUCTIONS:

Follow the prep technique next to each ingredient.

Cook pasta, following the package instructions. In a large skillet sauté portobello mushrooms, shallots, Swiss chard stalks, crushed red pepper and garlic with the olive oil. Add the vegetable broth and reduce to half. Add the Swiss chard and sauté until wilted. Fold in the cooked pasta and season with salt and pepper.

Serve with parmesan on the side.

CATEGORY TAGS:

- ○ gluten-free
- ○ high fiber
- ○ high protein
- ○ low calorie
- ◉ low carbohydrate / low sugar
- ◉ low cholesterol
- ○ low fat / low saturated fat
- ○ low sodium
- ◉ vegan
- ◉ vegetarian
- ◉ whole food plant based
- ◉ whole grain

NUTRITIONAL DATA:

calories	119.59
fat	3.32g
sat fat	3.58g
cholesterol	0mg
sodium	308.49mg
carbohydrates	19.60g
fiber	2.92g
sugars	2.31g
protein	3.81g

Polynesian Sweet and Sour Tofu

The delights of chameleon-like tofu, here spruced up with sweet, sour, hot and mellow flavors. There's almost a Polynesian flair to the taste, the contrast between tongue-awakening ginger, the spiciness of chili sauce and the fruity and bold notes of sweet and sour. Pineapple adds acid, peppers bring a subtle crunch, and the very quick cook leaves everything bright and recognizable to the eye and palate for an attractive and tasty dish. PS: Placing the tofu under a weighted plate to press out some of the moisture will result in a firmer texture and easier browning in the pan.

PREP INSTRUCTIONS:

Yield: 8 (1/2 cup) servings
Prep Time: 8 minutes

Cooking Time: 10 minutes
Total Time: 18 minutes

RECIPE INGREDIENTS:

1 block of firm tofu, pressed and cut into large cubes
1 ½ teaspoons sesame oil
1 ½ cups pineapple, cut into 1 inch cubes
½ cup green bell pepper, cut into 1 inch cubes
½ cup yellow or red onion, cut into 1 inch cubes
½ cup red bell pepper, cut into 1 inch cubes

1 tablespoon fresh garlic, minced
1 tablespoon fresh ginger, minced
2 ½ cups sweet and sour sauce
2 tablespoons sweet chili sauce
Water for stir-frying
Optional topping – sesame seeds

INSTRUCTIONS:

Follow the prep technique next to each ingredient.

In a hot wok or sauté pan, add the sesame oil followed by the pineapple and caramelize until golden. Add the onions and peppers and cook until edges start to brown, adding water to avoid burning. Add the ginger and garlic and sauté until fragrant. Fold in the tofu and cook until edges are caramelized. Add the sweet and sour sauce and bring to a simmer and mix in the sweet chili sauce. Serve over brown rice and top with sesame seeds if desired.

CATEGORY TAGS:

- ◉ gluten-free
- ○ high fiber
- ○ high protein
- ○ low calorie
- ◉ low carbohydrate / low sugar
- ◉ low cholesterol
- ○ low fat / low saturated fat
- ◉ low sodium
- ◉ vegan
- ◉ vegetarian
- ◉ whole food plant based
- ◉ whole grain

NUTRITIONAL DATA:

calories	107.59
fat	3.50g
sat fat	0.46g
cholesterol	0mg
sodium	57.80mg
carbohydrates	16.21g
fiber	1.20g
sugars	12.03g
protein	4.95g

Cumin and Garlic Roasted Chicken

Imagine an evening in the Casbah after preparing and serving this bit of Marrakesh. It's the combination of cumin with its woody taste, fragrance and digestion-aiding properties; the quick flash of heat from cayenne pepper, and the slightly citrusy, high antioxidant cilantro, that brings such an exotic taste and great health benefits to the chicken, and what keeps it moist in the oven. Serve with fragrant jasmine rice or in a pita for a quick vacation to Morocco.

PREP INSTRUCTIONS:

Yield: 9 (4 oz) servings
Prep Time: 8 minutes

Cooking Time: 15 minutes
Total Time: 23 minutes

RECIPE INGREDIENTS:

9 (4 oz) chicken breasts
2 garlic cloves, peeled
¼ cup fresh cilantro, chopped
½ teaspoon kosher salt
⅛ teaspoon cayenne pepper
1 ½ teaspoons paprika
1 ½ teaspoons ground cumin
2 tablespoons olive oil
2 tablespoons fresh parsley, chopped
1 bunch scallions, chopped

INSTRUCTIONS:

Follow the prep technique next to each ingredient.

Preheat oven to 350°F. Prepare pan with nonstick cooking oil.

Combine the scallions, garlic, cilantro, parsley, salt, paprika, cayenne, cumin and olive oil in food processor and mince. Pat dry the chicken breasts and place in a bowl. Fold in the condiment mixture. Let stand at least 1 hour. Roast chicken on a prepared sheet pan for 12 to 15 minutes or until it reaches an internal temperature of 165 degrees.

CATEGORY TAGS:

- ◉ gluten-free
- ○ high fiber
- ○ high protein
- ○ low calorie
- ◉ low carbohydrate / low sugar
- ○ low cholesterol
- ○ low fat / low saturated fat
- ○ low sodium
- ○ vegan
- ○ vegetarian
- ○ whole food plant based
- ○ whole grain

NUTRITIONAL DATA:

calories	171.32
fat	7.25g
sat fat	1.79g
cholesterol	66.67mg
sodium	145.36mg
carbohydrates	0.82g
fiber	0.37g
sugars	0.13g
protein	25.57g

Havana Mojito Chicken with Hot Pepper and Lime Dressing

Taking a cue from the classic Cuban drink, this dish adds lime, mint and brown sugar to a chicken marinade, leaning on the fragrant tang of lime and sweetness of the brown sugar to flavor the dish. Don't be tempted to use bottled lime juice (too much sugar) or dried mint, which never has the aromatic oils of fresh leaves and stems— that's right, never waste the stems. Flavor-rich marinades are a simple way to enhance chicken without adding salt or sugar-filled dressings.

PREP INSTRUCTIONS:

Yield: 8 (4oz) servings
Prep Time: 5 minutes

Cooking Time: 15-20 minutes
Total Time: 25 minutes

RECIPE INGREDIENTS:

8- 4 oz. chicken breast
1 tablespoon lime zest
¼ cup lime juice
3 tablespoons fresh mint, chopped
1 jalapeno, seeded and chopped

1 medium yellow onion
1 teaspoon brown sugar
1 tablespoon fresh garlic, chopped
¼ teaspoon Spanish paprika

INSTRUCTIONS:

Follow the prep technique next to each ingredient.

Preheat oven to 350°F.

In a food processor combine the ingredients except the chicken and blend well. Pour over chicken and marinade for at least 2 hours. On a sprayed sheet pan, roast the chicken for 15 minutes or until its internal temperature reaches 165F.

CATEGORY TAGS:

- ◉ gluten-free
- ○ high fiber
- ○ high protein
- ○ low calorie
- ◉ low carbohydrate / low sugar
- ○ low cholesterol
- ◉ low fat / low saturated fat
- ○ low sodium
- ○ vegan
- ○ vegetarian
- ○ whole food plant based
- ○ whole grain

NUTRITIONAL DATA:

calories	138
fat	2.10g
sat fat	1.03g
cholesterol	75.94mg
sodium	258.10mg
carbohydrates	4.07g
fiber	0.63g
sugars	1.91g
protein	26.75g

Creole Spiced Marinated Chicken

An often-overlooked cooking technique, marinating chicken or beef not only introduces new flavors to occasionally uninteresting ingredients, but naturally tenderizes the meat. Chicken blooms from a stay in lemon and garlic, while the trio of coriander, cumin and peppers perfects the taste by adding a Creole touch. Serve as shown in a pita, over pasta, or cooled down with slaw and a touch of salsa. Remember to marinate in the refrigerator, and discard used marinade instead of reusing.

PREP INSTRUCTIONS:

Yield: 4 (4oz) servings
Prep Time: 10 minutes

Cooking Time: 15 minutes for spiced chicken
Total Time: 25 minutes

RECIPE INGREDIENTS:

4- 4 oz. chicken breast
¼ teaspoon olive oil
1 teaspoon ground cumin
1 teaspoon paprika
¼ teaspoon cayenne

¾ teaspoon ground coriander
2 teaspoons fresh garlic, chopped
1/2 teaspoon kosher salt
2-3 tablespoons, lemon juice
Nonstick cooking spray

INSTRUCTIONS:

Follow the prep technique next to each ingredient.

Preheat oven to 350˚F.

Blend all ingredients together and marinade with the chicken at least 3 hours before cooking. Place chicken on a prepared sheet pan with nonstick cooking spray or parchment paper. Roast chicken for 15 to 20 minutes or until internal temperature reaches 165 degrees.

This recipe is one of the components for the Mediterranean Wrap with Chicken.

CATEGORY TAGS:

- ◉ gluten-free
- ○ high fiber
- ○ high protein
- ○ low calorie
- ◉ low carbohydrate / low sugar
- ○ low cholesterol
- ○ low fat / low saturated fat
- ○ low sodium
- ○ vegan
- ○ vegetarian
- ○ whole food plant based
- ○ whole grain

NUTRITIONAL DATA:

calories	143.83
fat	3.18g
sat fat	0.79g
cholesterol	67.23mg
sodium	176.74mg
carbohydrates	1.85g
fiber	0.53g
sugars	0.31g
protein	25.63g

Mediterranean Roasted Chicken and Veggie Wrap with From-Scratch Hummus

The secret is in the flavorings, a richly seasoned hummus, alive with tastes of the Mediterranean, chicken marinated with fragrant cumin and paprika, and the freshness of juicy cucumber and fresh vegetables. Give the tortilla a quick toast in a dry skillet or pop them in the oven for the last minute of cooking to make it easier to wrap and a fresher, toastier wrap.

PREP INSTRUCTIONS:

Yield: 6 (1/2 portion) servings
Prep Time: 15 minutes

Cooking Time: 20 minutes
Total Time: 35 minutes

RECIPE INGREDIENTS:

3 whole grain tortilla wraps, 12 inches
1 small cucumber, julienned
1 red bell pepper, julienned
¾ cup carrot, julienned

4 ½ cups baby spinach
3 - ¼ cup portions of Homemade Garbanzo Hummus, (page 188)
3 portions of Creole Spiced Marinated Chicken, (page 148)

INSTRUCTIONS:

Follow the prep technique next to each ingredient

***Review recipe for Creole Spiced Marinated Chicken and Homemade Garbanzo Hummus**

To make the wraps, place tortilla on a flat surface, add the hummus in the center of the wrap spreading the mixture sideways, leaving two inches on both sides of the tortilla. Place the cucumber strips, follow with red bell pepper and carrots. Slice the chicken (making sure the chicken has cooled down) and place one serving on top of the vegetables, follow with spinach. As you cover the mixture in the center, fold in the sides and roll the wrap away from you. Cut in two portions. Repeat the same procedure for each.

CATEGORY TAGS:

O gluten-free
◉ high fiber
O high protein
O low calorie
◉ low carbohydrate / low sugar
O low cholesterol
O low fat / low saturated fat
O low sodium
O vegan
O vegetarian
O whole food plant based
◉ whole grain

NUTRITIONAL DATA:

calories	241.49
fat	5.94g
sat fat	1.30g
cholesterol	33.62mg
sodium	498.17mg
carbohydrates	27.39g
fiber	7.23g
sugars	4.13g
protein	19.20g

Scandinavian Mustard-Roasted Salmon

Mustard on salmon makes for a very Scandinavian dish, with a fine flavor of rosemary and lemon peeking through the mellow layer of mustard. Salmon is a perfect source of omega-3 fatty acids, crucial for a healthy metabolism. Find the best coarse-ground mustard on the supermarket shelf—an adventurous soul might even try a spicy Creole variety from Louisiana—or a smoother Dijon for subtler flavor. Served with thinly sliced cucumber and a dollop of sour cream, this dish will find a home at your next smorgasbord. Skol!

PREP INSTRUCTIONS:

Yield: 6 (3 oz) servings
Prep Time: 5 minutes

Cooking Time: 12 minutes
Total Time: 17 minutes

RECIPE INGREDIENTS:

18 oz. fresh salmon, cut into 6 (3oz) servings
1 tablespoon shallots, minced
1 tablespoon spicy brown mustard
1 teaspoon lemon zest
1 tablespoon lemon juice
2 teaspoons fresh garlic, minced
1 teaspoon rosemary, chopped
1 teaspoon fresh Italian parsley, chopped
¾ teaspoon fine ground black pepper

INSTRUCTIONS:

Follow the prep technique next to each ingredient.

Preheat oven to 350˚F. Prepare pan with nonstick cooking oil.

Mix all the ingredients together except the salmon to make the mustard spread. Spread evenly on top of each portion. Place fish on a prepared sheet pan and bake 12- 15 minutes.

CATEGORY TAGS:

- ◉ gluten-free
- ○ high fiber
- ○ high protein
- ○ low calorie
- ◉ low carbohydrate / low sugar
- ◉ low cholesterol
- ○ low fat / low saturated fat
- ◉ low sodium
- ○ vegan
- ○ vegetarian
- ○ whole food plant based
- ○ whole grain

NUTRITIONAL DATA:

calories	183.66
fat	11.44g
sat fat	2.60g
cholesterol	46.78mg
sodium	75.79mg
carbohydrates	1.04g
fiber	0.21g
sugars	0.22g
protein	17.52g

Portobello Eggplant Napoleon

Packed with nutrition, this lovely layered feast offers a different taste combination with every bite. The meatiness of roasted vegetables and tofu brings an earthy quality that will make the family forget there isn't any actual meat involved. The combination of basil, thyme and parsley give this "Napoleon" a French flavor; make extra to serve tableside. And by thinly slicing the zucchini and eggplant lengthwise, this meal could also be served as a veggie lasagna.

PREP INSTRUCTIONS:

Yield: 4 servings
Prep Time: 10 minutes

Cooking Time: 20 minutes
Total Time: 30 minutes

RECIPE INGREDIENTS:

1 cup zucchini, sliced bias
8 oz. tofu, sliced sideways into four slabs
1 large tomato, cut into 4 thick slices
6 oz. pimiento pepper, cut into 4 pieces

8 oz. eggplant, sliced into four disks
4 portobello mushrooms, gills removed
½ oz. fresh herb balsamic vinaigrette, recipe follows

For the Fresh Herb Balsamic Vinaigrette:

½ teaspoon fresh garlic, minced
1 tablespoon fresh basil, chopped
1 tablespoon fresh thyme, chopped
1 tablespoon fresh parsley, chopped

½ teaspoon kosher salt
½ teaspoon fine ground pepper
¾ cup balsamic vinegar
3 tablespoons olive oil

INSTRUCTIONS:

Follow the prep technique next to each ingredient.

Preheat oven to 350°F. Prepare pan with nonstick cooking oil.

On a prepared sheet pan spray zucchini, eggplant, tofu and tomatoes. Place in the oven and roast for 15 minutes. Remove from the oven and build the vegetable napoleon as desired adding the pimiento pepper. Place back in the oven and roast for 5 more minutes. Remove from the oven and drizzle with the fresh herb balsamic vinaigrette. Serve hot.

CATEGORY TAGS:

- ◉ gluten-free
- ◉ high fiber
- ○ high protein
- ○ low calorie
- ◉ low carbohydrate / low sugar
- ◉ low cholesterol
- ○ low fat / low saturated fat
- ○ low sodium
- ◉ vegan
- ◉ vegetarian
- ◉ whole food plant based
- ○ whole grain

NUTRITIONAL DATA:

calories	153.54
fat	5.38g
sat fat	0.47g
cholesterol	0mg
sodium	188.62mg
carbohydrates	17.14g
fiber	5.71g
sugars	7.92g
protein	9.17g

Simple Catalan Tomato Sauce for Fish

Barcelona is known for architecture, late-night entertainment, and food that is simple, fresh and very, very good. The Catalan diet depends on the staples of north-east Spain; olives, plump tomatoes, and some of the best olive oil in the world. This simple but very flavorful (and healthy) tomato sauce will complement any firm, white fish, adding a savory, tangy dimension to what might otherwise be a bland dish. Go the extra step and use the best, smooth-tasting olive oil you can find!

PREP INSTRUCTIONS:

Yield: 8 servings
Prep Time: 10 minutes

Cooking Time: 10 minutes
Total Time: 20 minutes

RECIPE INGREDIENTS:

1 tablespoon olive oil
1 tablespoon fresh garlic, thinly sliced or minced
1 cup yellow onion, diced
1 bay leaf
½ teaspoon dried oregano
⅛ teaspoon crushed red pepper
¼ teaspoon fine ground black pepper
1 teaspoon fresh thyme, chopped

1 tablespoon fresh oregano, chopped
¼ cup Kalamata olives, sliced
1 tablespoon capers, drained
1 tablespoon golden balsamic vinegar
3 cups diced tomatoes in juice
1 cup water
2 tablespoons fresh Italian parsley, chopped
32 ounces of fresh cod, cut into 8 portions

INSTRUCTIONS:

Follow the prep technique next to each ingredient.

In a small saucepan heat the olive oil at a medium heat and sauté onions until translucent, adding the garlic, bay leaf, oregano, thyme, red pepper flakes and the vinegar. Add the rest of the ingredients and simmer for 6 to 10 minutes. Can be made in advance.

In a large skillet with a lid, pan sear the cod loins and add sauce. Cover and simmer until cod loins are cooked through, about 10 to 12 minutes.

CATEGORY TAGS:

◉ gluten-free
○ high fiber
○ high protein
○ low calorie
◉ low carbohydrate / low sugar
◉ low cholesterol
○ low fat / low saturated fat
○ low sodium
○ vegan
○ vegetarian
○ whole food plant based
○ whole grain

NUTRITIONAL DATA:

calories	148.71
fat	3.19
sat fat	0.41g
cholesterol	48.76mg
sodium	341.31mg
carbohydrates	7.55g
fiber	1.97g
sugars	2.37g
protein	21.36g

VEGETABLES

Persian Inspired Cumin Roasted Carrots

Everyone has had a child turn up their nose at carrots—and truthfully, some adults as well. This may be the answer: sweet, slow roasted until the sugars rise and caramelize for a lovely brown sear and slightly nutty taste. Mixing those flavors with cumin is only natural—both the root vegetable and cumin seeds originate in Persia, and are both mentioned in the Bible. Cumin adds a mild spiciness, musky, slightly licorice aroma and high levels of vitamins, minerals and antioxidants to anything.

PREP INSTRUCTIONS:

Yield: 6 (1/2 cup) servings
Prep Time: 7 minutes

Cooking Time: 30 minutes
Total Time: 37 minutes

RECIPE INGREDIENTS:

4 cups carrots, bias cut
1 ½ teaspoons extra virgin olive oil
1 ½ teaspoons cumin seeds, toasted
½ teaspoon fine ground black pepper
½ teaspoon ground cinnamon
Nonstick cooking spray

INSTRUCTIONS:

Follow the prep technique next to each ingredient. Pre-heat oven to 350˚F.

In a large bowl combine all ingredients and toss to coat. Spread carrots in a single layer on baking sheet pan prepared with cooking spray. Roast carrots 25 to 30 minutes, turning carrots once until golden brown or caramelized.

CATEGORY TAGS:

- ◉ gluten-free
- ○ high fiber
- ○ high protein
- ○ low calorie
- ◉ low carbohydrate / low sugar
- ◉ low cholesterol
- ◉ low fat / low saturated fat
- ◉ low sodium
- ◉ vegan
- ◉ vegetarian
- ◉ whole food plant based
- ○ whole grain

NUTRITIONAL DATA:

calories	46.33
fat	1.49g
sat fat	0.21g
cholesterol	0mg
sodium	57.06mg
carbohydrates	8.32g
fiber	2.50g
sugars	3.87g
protein	0.88g

Quick Broccoli and Edamame Side Dish with Sweet and Savory Dressing

Every ingredient in this recipe shouts out its health benefits. The fact that it tastes good—and can be done in 11 minutes—is a bonus. Asian flavor profiles are represented well: the tartness of vinegar (an age-old health booster), sweet and savory marmalade, and a splash of spice from mustard bring out the slightly nutty, very green taste of edamame, a soybean variety that has been enjoyed in Asian cultures for centuries. There are even Japanese poems about it. The crunch of bright carrots and broccoli makes this a salad good for adults and kids alike.

PREP INSTRUCTIONS:

Yield: 8 (3/4 cup) servings
Prep Time: 5 minutes

Cooking Time: 6 minutes
Total Time: 11 minutes

RECIPE INGREDIENTS:

1 lb. broccoli florets
1 ½ cups edamame beans
1 cup carrots, julienned
6 tablespoons rice vinegar

2 tablespoons orange marmalade
1 ½ teaspoons fresh garlic, chopped
1 ½ teaspoons country style mustard

INSTRUCTIONS:

Follow the prep technique next to each ingredient.

In a small saucepan combine the vinegar, marmalade, garlic and mustard. Simmer until all flavors are well combined. Place the broccoli and edamame in a steam basket and cook 2-3 minutes. Remove from heat and combine with the shredded carrots, folding in the orange marmalade-mustard mixture.

CATEGORY TAGS:

- ◉ gluten-free
- ◉ high fiber
- ○ high protein
- ○ low calorie
- ◉ low carbohydrate / low sugar
- ◉ low cholesterol
- ◉ low fat / low saturated fat
- ◉ low sodium
- ◉ vegan
- ◉ vegetarian
- ◉ whole food plant based
- ○ whole grain

NUTRITIONAL DATA:

calories	53.30
fat	1.28g
sat fat	0.04g
cholesterol	0mg
sodium	38.50mg
carbohydrates	8.00g
fiber	3.20g
sugars	2.53g
protein	4.13g

Fast and Flavorful Spanish Green Beans

Fast, controlled cooking is the key for great green beans, full of phytonutrients and antioxidants. If you cook too quickly, older beans will have a woody, unappetizing taste; cook too long and the beans will be so soft you might as well open a can. A short steam will bring out the dazzling color and crisp, garden-fresh taste. Fresh green beans and tomato are a classic Spanish combination and an easy way to add a healthy vegetable to the table. Pick the smallest, sweetest beans available for an appetizing dish that looks great as well.

PREP INSTRUCTIONS:

Yield: 6 (3/4 cup) servings
Prep Time: 6 minutes

Cooking Time: 6 minutes
Total Time: 12 minutes

RECIPE INGREDIENTS:

8 oz. fresh green beans, snipped
2/3 cup yellow onions, diced
1/3 cup green pepper, diced
1 ½ teaspoons olive oil

2 plum tomato, chopped
1 tablespoon fresh basil, chopped
1 teaspoon fresh rosemary, chopped
¼ teaspoon kosher salt

INSTRUCTIONS:

Follow the prep technique next to each ingredient.

Steam green beans to al dente; set aside. Sauté onions and peppers in olive oil until soft. Add plum tomatoes, fresh herbs and steamed green beans. Sauté to incorporate the flavors.

CATEGORY TAGS:

- ◉ gluten-free
- ○ high fiber
- ○ high protein
- ◉ low calorie
- ◉ low carbohydrate / low sugar
- ◉ low cholesterol
- ◉ low fat / low saturated fat
- ◉ low sodium
- ◉ vegan
- ◉ vegetarian
- ◉ whole food plant based
- ○ whole grain

NUTRITIONAL DATA:

calories	35.25
fat	1.32g
sat fat	0.20g
cholesterol	0mg
sodium	84.26mg
carbohydrates	5.71g
fiber	1.84g
sugars	3.13g
protein	1.23g

No Fuss Cauliflower and Spinach Sauté

Cauliflower is a much-neglected vegetable, but this quick hit of vital nutrition (the health benefits of brassicas like cauliflower, cabbage and broccoli are well documented) makes a simple side dish, and the combination of florets and flavorful ingredients such as garlic and shallots enhances the subtle taste. Look for the green, spiraled Romanesco variety for some visual excitement, and if you have time, pop the cauliflower onto an oven sheet with a light drizzle of oil and roast for 20 minutes before adding to the dish; you'll have a new appreciation for this versatile ingredient.

PREP INSTRUCTIONS:

Yield: 6 (3/4 cup) servings
Prep Time: 5 minutes

Cooking Time: 10 minutes
Total Time: 15 minutes

RECIPE INGREDIENTS:

1 ¾ teaspoons olive oil
¼ cup shallots, sliced
1 ½ tablespoons fresh garlic, minced
1 ¼ cups baby spinach

6 cups raw cauliflower florets
1 tablespoon lemon juice
⅛ teaspoon kosher salt
¼ teaspoon white pepper

INSTRUCTIONS:

Follow the prep technique next to each ingredient.

Add spinach and ¼ cup water to small saucepan with a lid. Cover and simmer until spinach collapses and wilts. Remove and shock in cold water. Steam cauliflower in a steam basket and set aside.

In a medium-size skillet sauté the shallots and garlic with the oil; add the cauliflower and the spinach and sauté for a few more minutes. Season with salt and pepper. Remove from heat and fold in the lemon juice.

CATEGORY TAGS:

- ◉ gluten-free
- ○ high fiber
- ○ high protein
- ○ low calorie
- ◉ low carbohydrate / low sugar
- ◉ low cholesterol
- ◉ low fat / low saturated fat
- ◉ low sodium
- ◉ vegan
- ◉ vegetarian
- ◉ whole food plant based
- ○ whole grain

NUTRITIONAL DATA:

calories	49.90
fat	1.39g
sat fat	0.20g
cholesterol	0mg
sodium	80.63mg
carbohydrates	7.72g
fiber	2.74g
sugars	2.61g
protein	2.76g

Roasted French Eggplant, Squash and Pepper Ratatouille

The name Ratatouille might be familiar from a popular animated movie, but the dish itself could seem uncommon. This vegetable stew from Provence is a fairly simple dish combining peppers, onions, squash and large amounts of those two related powerhouses, tomatoes and eggplant, providing a rich mixture of phytonutrients and antioxidants that may aid in cholesterol regulation. Roasting the vegetables before combining adds a new, marvelously rich twist to this traditionally slow-simmered delight.

PREP INSTRUCTIONS:

Yield: 8 (3/4 cup) servings
Prep Time: 10 minutes

Cooking Time: 20 minutes
Total Time: 30 minutes

RECIPE INGREDIENTS:

2 cups plum tomatoes, quartered
1 cup yellow squash, chopped
1 cup zucchini squash, chopped
1 cup red bell pepper, chopped
2 cups red onion, chopped
2 cups eggplant, chopped
2 teaspoons olive oil

1 ½ teaspoons fresh garlic, chopped
1 tablespoon fresh thyme
¾ teaspoon fine ground black pepper
1 teaspoon kosher salt
¼ cup fresh Italian parsley, chopped
¼ cup fresh basil, shredded

INSTRUCTIONS:

Follow the prep technique next to each ingredient.

Preheat oven to 350°F.

Combine the tomatoes, yellow and zucchini squash with half the olive oil, garlic, pepper, thyme and salt. Toss to coat and place on a sheet pan. Repeat the same procedure with the eggplant, red bell peppers and the red onions. Roast vegetables 15-20 minutes or until golden brown but firm. Remove from the oven and fold all vegetables together, adding the fresh parsley and basil. Serve.

CATEGORY TAGS:

- ◉ gluten-free
- ○ high fiber
- ○ high protein
- ○ low calorie
- ◉ low carbohydrate / low sugar
- ◉ low cholesterol
- ○ low fat / low saturated fat
- ○ low sodium
- ◉ vegan
- ◉ vegetarian
- ◉ whole food plant based
- ○ whole grain

NUTRITIONAL DATA:

calories	64.69
fat	2.84g
sat fat	0.66g
cholesterol	0mg
sodium	255.72mg
carbohydrates	9.22g
fiber	2.72g
sugars	4.51g
protein	1.80g

Slow Roasted Brussels Sprouts with Sautéed Cabbage, Spinach and Chard

If you've avoided Brussels sprouts, you probably have not had them roasted. The high heat of a roasting oven turns these little cabbages into one of nature's great delights: nutty, sweet, with the occasional crunchy browned edge. Matched with the depth of flavor of browned onions and tart cranberries, sprouts are a treat by themselves, but added to the combo of vitamin and mineral-rich greens they become a low calorie delight that is good for you as well.

PREP INSTRUCTIONS:

Yield: 8 (3/4 cup) servings
Prep Time: 10 minutes

Cooking Time: 40 minutes
Total Time: 50 minutes

RECIPE INGREDIENTS:

3 tablespoons olive oil
½ cups red onions, julienned
1 tablespoon fresh garlic, minced
4 tablespoons dried cranberries
¼ cup balsamic vinegar
12 oz. fresh brussels sprouts

2 cups red cabbage, shredded
2 cups power greens (baby spinach, baby red and green Swiss chard, baby kale)
¼ teaspoon salt
½ teaspoon kosher salt
nonstick cooking spray

INSTRUCTIONS:

Follow the prep technique next to each ingredient. Preheat oven to 350 ° F.

Trim and cut the brussels sprouts in half. Coat with nonstick cooking spray and roast 20 to 30 minutes or until golden brown; if you prefer them steamed, place in a steam basket for 6 to 8 minutes. In hot skillet sauté onion in olive oil and add half of the balsamic vinegar to caramelize the onions. Follow with the dried cranberries and roasted brussels sprouts. Add the garlic and sauté to coat. Season with salt and pepper. Fold in the rest of the ingredients and the remaining balsamic vinegar. Sauté until vegetables are wilted but firm.

CATEGORY TAGS:

- ◉ gluten-free
- ○ high fiber
- ○ high protein
- ○ low calorie
- ◉ low carbohydrate / low sugar
- ◉ low cholesterol
- ○ low fat / low saturated fat
- ◉ low sodium
- ◉ vegan
- ◉ vegetarian
- ◉ whole food plant based
- ○ whole grain

NUTRITIONAL DATA:

calories	107.78
fat	5.60g
sat fat	0.78g
cholesterol	0mg
sodium	101.29mg
carbohydrates	12.52g
fiber	2.94g
sugars	6.80g
protein	2.12g

SPREADS & SAUCES

Sweet, Tangy and Spicy Mango Salsa

So quick, so easy, so delicious. This is a classic marriage of sweet fruit, tangy lemon and spicy pepper that awakens every part of the tongue, and will be a great seasoning for chicken, fish, or roasted tofu dishes. With so many different varieties of mangos (there are hundreds), it might be hard to pick the right one: fresh mangoes don't have to be red to be ready—even a green mango can be perfectly ripe. Rather smell for a sweet, almost pineapple aroma and a bit of softness under the skin.

PREP INSTRUCTIONS:

Yield: 12 (1/4 cup) servings
Prep Time: 8 minutes
Cooking Time: 0
Total Time: 8 minutes

RECIPE INGREDIENTS:

3-4 cups mango, diced
¾ cup red bell pepper, diced
½ cup scallions, thinly sliced
4 tablespoons cilantro, chopped
 pinch cayenne pepper
2 tablespoons freshly squeezed orange juice
½ teaspoon lemon zest

INSTRUCTIONS:

Follow the prep technique next to each ingredient.

Combine all ingredients together and mix well.

CATEGORY TAGS:

- ◉ gluten-free
- ○ high fiber
- ○ high protein
- ○ low calorie
- ◉ low carbohydrate / low sugar
- ◉ low cholesterol
- ◉ low fat / low saturated fat
- ◉ low sodium
- ◉ vegan
- ◉ vegetarian
- ◉ whole food plant based
- ○ whole grain

NUTRITIONAL DATA:

calories	0
fat	0.26g
sat fat	0.05g
cholesterol	0mg
sodium	1.85mg
carbohydrates	9.51g
fiber	1.22g
sugars	8.14g
protein	0.66g

Quick Pineapple Salsa with Jalapeño

A twist on an old favorite, using pineapple instead of tomato in a salsa. In fact, "salsa" is just another word for sauce, and traditional Latin salsa condiments can use all manner of ingredients, from tomatoes and chili peppers to avocado, carrots and even chocolate. Choose a healthy-looking, ripe pineapple (an appetizing, sweet smell is the best test) or use canned -- either way will provide a sweet lift to a delightful array of dishes or as a dip without adding processed sugar to our diet.

PREP INSTRUCTIONS:

Yield: 12 (1/4 cup) servings
Prep Time: 8 minutes
Cooking Time: 0 minutes
Total Time: 8 minutes

RECIPE INGREDIENTS:

1 lb. or 3 cups pineapple, diced
1 cup red bell pepper, diced
1 small red onion, diced
2 small jalapeño peppers, minced
2 tablespoons Italian parsley, chopped

INSTRUCTIONS:

Follow the prep technique next to each ingredient.

Combine all ingredients together, mix well and serve.

CATEGORY TAGS:

- ◉ gluten-free
- ○ high fiber
- ○ high protein
- ◉ low calorie
- ◉ low carbohydrate / low sugar
- ○ low cholesterol
- ◉ low fat / low saturated fat
- ◉ low sodium
- ◉ vegan
- ◉ vegetarian
- ◉ whole food plant based
- ○ whole grain

NUTRITIONAL DATA:

calories	26.44
fat	0.10g
sat fat	0.01g
cholesterol	0mg
sodium	1.66mg
carbohydrates	6.53g
fiber	0.98g
sugars	4.47g
protein	0.46g

Bright Edamame Bean Hummus

In the past few years, we've become rather enamored of hummus, that Middle Eastern delight made from chickpeas, olive oil and tahini that is so important to that area's food culture that ownership rights have been heatedly debated. But when you think about it, chickpeas are just another, very tasty legume – so why not try the others? Edamame, another fruit of exotic lands, has become a popular snack item, and the bright green look and taste of young soybeans is ideal for a smooth paste, and actually easier to accomplish than the sometimes stubborn garbanzo. Try adding a touch of sesame oil for an Asian flair.

PREP INSTRUCTIONS:

Yield: 4 (1/2 cup) servings
Prep Time: 5 minutes
Cooking Time: 5 minutes
Total Time: 10 minutes

RECIPE INGREDIENTS:

2 cups edamame beans
3 tablespoons fresh lemon juice
2 ½ tablespoons olive or canola oil
2 teaspoons fresh garlic, minced
1/2 teaspoon cumin
1/4 teaspoon cayenne pepper
3 tablespoons water
1/4 teaspoon kosher salt

INSTRUCTIONS:

Measure ingredients and chop garlic.

Place all ingredients except water in a food processor. Let the mixture break down enough before adding the water so the mixture has a smooth instead of a coarse consistency.

CATEGORY TAGS:

- ◉ gluten-free
- ◉ high fiber
- ○ high protein
- ○ low calorie
- ◉ low carbohydrate / low sugar
- ◉ low cholesterol
- ○ low fat / low saturated fat
- ◉ low sodium
- ◉ vegan
- ◉ vegetarian
- ◉ whole food plant based
- ○ whole grain

NUTRITIONAL DATA:

calories	148
fat	12g
sat fat	0.65g
cholesterol	0mg
sodium	125mg
carbohydrates	7g
fiber	3g
sugars	1.78g
protein	6g

Quick Chop Rustic Tomato Salsa

This is as simple as it gets: a rustic, fast chop of vegetables and the barest kiss of extra flavor make for a supreme salsa. The small ingredient list and minimal preparation demand the freshest, brightest tomatoes; haunt your local farmer's market or farm stand for something vine-ripened, and if tomatoes aren't in season locally—wait until they are!

PREP INSTRUCTIONS:

Yield: 5 (1/4 cup) servings
Prep Time: 5 minutes
Cooking Time: 0 minutes
Total Time: 5 minutes

RECIPE INGREDIENTS:

1 jalapeno, chopped
3 tablespoons red onions, diced
1 tablespoon cilantro, chopped
1 tablespoon lime juice
1 cup tomatoes, diced
1/16 teaspoon salt

INSTRUCTIONS:

Follow the prep technique next to each ingredient.

Combine all ingredients and mix well.

CATEGORY TAGS:

- ◉ gluten-free
- ○ high fiber
- ○ high protein
- ◉ low calorie
- ◉ low carbohydrate / low sugar
- ◉ low cholesterol
- ◉ low fat / low saturated fat
- ◉ low sodium
- ◉ vegan
- ◉ vegetarian
- ◉ whole food plant based
- ○ whole grain

NUTRITIONAL DATA:

calories	16.01
fat	0.02g
sat fat	0.01g
cholesterol	0mg
sodium	128.48mg
carbohydrates	3.40g
fiber	0.49mg
sugars	2.02g
protein	0.51g

Stove Top Cinnamon Cranberry Sauce

It might be tempting to buy that perennial can of jellied cranberries—there might be one left over from Thanksgivings past in your cupboard right now—but there's really no comparison between that and this handmade supper trimming. Just watching the magic as it jells might be enough. And don't limit its uses to a turkey dinner or leftover sandwich; the tart character of cranberry sauce lends itself to experimentation. Spoon it over yogurt for a morning pick-me-up; mix it into a pound cake recipe; use it as a topping for burgers or waffles or add it to ketchup for a tangy dip for barbecue.

PREP INSTRUCTIONS:

Yield: 14 (3 Tablespoons) servings
Prep Time: 3 minutes
Cooking Time: 5 minutes
Total Time: 8 minutes

RECIPE INGREDIENTS:

1 (12oz) bag of fresh cranberries
¾ cup maple syrup
⅓ cup fresh squeezed orange juice
1 teaspoon orange zest
½ cup orange segments
1 cinnamon stick

INSTRUCTIONS:

Combine the cranberries, maple syrup, orange juice and cinnamon stick in a 3-qt. saucepan and bring to a boil. Reduce the heat to medium low and simmer, stirring occasionally, just until the cranberries burst, about 5 minutes. Remove from the heat, stir in the zest and the orange segments and let cool to room temperature. The sauce will thicken as it cools.

CATEGORY TAGS:

- ◉ gluten-free
- ○ high fiber
- ○ high protein
- ○ low calorie
- ◉ low carbohydrate / low sugar
- ◉ low cholesterol
- ◉ low fat / low saturated fat
- ◉ low sodium
- ◉ vegan
- ◉ vegetarian
- ◉ whole food plant based
- ○ whole grain

NUTRITIONAL DATA:

calories	65.19
fat	0.03g
sat fat	0.00g
cholesterol	0mg
sodium	2.18mg
carbohydrates	15.89g
fiber	0.20g
sugars	12.43g
protein	0.11g

Puerto Rican Pepper, Onion and Garlic Sofrito

There are certain food combinations that become the basis for an entire cuisine. The Cajun cooking of New Orleans depends on the trinity of celery, bell pepper and onion; the French live on a base of sautéed onion, shallot and finely chopped mushrooms called duxelles; and southern Indian cooks would be lost without a paste of ground ginger and garlic. Sofrito is the foundation upon which much of Puerto Rican and Latin American cooking is based, and adds a pop of flavor without additional salt. Cooked over low heat with oil (sofrito means lightly fried), the combination of peppers, onions and garlic release a glorious aroma and rich flavors, which only get better with time. Use as a base for beans, rice dishes or soups, or use as a condiment.

PREP INSTRUCTIONS:

Yield: 26 (1/3 cup) servings
Prep Time: 8 minutes

Cooking Time: 0
Total Time: 8 minutes

RECIPE INGREDIENTS:

3 cups yellow onions, diced
4 ½ cups green peppers, diced
3 cups red bell pepper, diced
6-9 garlic cloves
1 bunch cilantro
2 bay leaves
1 tablespoon fresh thyme

INSTRUCTIONS:

Follow the prep technique next to each ingredient.

In a food processor, place all ingredients and blend to a chunky consistency.

CATEGORY TAGS:

- ⦿ gluten-free
- ◯ high fiber
- ◯ high protein
- ⦿ low calorie
- ⦿ low carbohydrate / low sugar
- ⦿ low cholesterol
- ⦿ low fat / low saturated fat
- ⦿ low sodium
- ⦿ vegan
- ⦿ vegetarian
- ⦿ whole food plant based
- ◯ whole grain

NUTRITIONAL DATA:

calories	19.89
fat	0.13g
sat fat	0.03g
cholesterol	0mg
sodium	2.96mg
carbohydrates	4.39g
fiber	1.18g
sugars	2.11g
protein	0.69g

8-minute Corn and Red Pepper Salsa

Once this corn salsa is in your repertoire, it will find its way into dips, salads and chili, the sweet corn balancing the savory pepper and onion combination and tempering the spicy jalapeño. No cooking involved here, so nothing can beat this salsa for a last-minute highlight to almost any meal. Frozen corn is often crisper than canned, and if fresh corn is in season, cut it right off the cob for a special treat.

PREP INSTRUCTIONS:

Yield: 5 (1/2 cup) servings
Prep Time: 8 minutes
Cooking Time: 0
Total Time: 8 minutes

RECIPE INGREDIENTS:

1 ½ cups corn
½ cup red bell pepper, diced
½ cup red onion, diced
¼ teaspoon fresh jalapeño, chopped
½ teaspoon fresh garlic, minced
2 tablespoons cilantro, chopped
2 ½ tablespoons fresh lime juice
a pinch chipotle powder
a pinch chili powder
a pinch ground cumin

INSTRUCTIONS:

Follow the prep technique next to each ingredient.

Combine all ingredients. Refrigerate until ready to use. Salsa may be served at room temperature.

CATEGORY TAGS:

- ◉ gluten-free
- ○ high fiber
- ○ high protein
- ○ low calorie
- ◉ low carbohydrate / low sugar
- ◉ low cholesterol
- ◉ low fat / low saturated fat
- ○ low sodium
- ◉ vegan
- ◉ vegetarian
- ◉ whole food plant based
- ◉ whole grain

NUTRITIONAL DATA:

calories	43.27
fat	0.69g
sat fat	0.11g
cholesterol	0mg
sodium	76.04mg
carbohydrates	8.32g
fiber	0.41g
sugars	0.95g
protein	1.26g

Homemade Garbanzo Hummus

Store-bought hummus has become so popular (and such a big business) that it can be found almost anywhere. But it is a simple preparation and there's no reason not to make it at home—not to mention the difference in cost. A staple for breakfast, lunch and dinner in the Middle East, hummus is marvelously healthy. Chickpeas are a superb source of insoluble fiber and antioxidants plus being helpful for cholesterol regulation. The secret to great hummus? Patience; when the garbanzo paste looks like it is ready, process it just a little longer for a smooth texture, and reserve some of the liquid to moisten the hummus while it spins.

PREP INSTRUCTIONS:

Yield: 12 (1/3 cup) servings
Prep Time: 10 minutes

Cooking Time: 0
Total Time: 10 minutes

RECIPE INGREDIENTS:

4 cups of canned garbanzos, drained (reserve liquid)
½ teaspoon olive oil
1 tablespoon garlic, minced
1 ½ tablespoons tahini paste
¾ teaspoon cumin
½ teaspoon paprika
1 teaspoon chili powder
⅛ teaspoon cayenne pepper
½ cup garbanzo liquid or ½ cup water
1 tablespoon lemon juice
2 tablespoons Italian parsley, chopped

INSTRUCTIONS:

Follow the prep technique next to each ingredient.

In a food processor place the drained garbanzo beans with the rest of the ingredients and purée, adding liquid until smooth.

CATEGORY TAGS:

- ◉ gluten-free
- ◉ high fiber
- ○ high protein
- ○ low calorie
- ◉ low carbohydrate / low sugar
- ◉ low cholesterol
- ◉ low fat / low saturated fat
- ◉ low sodium
- ◉ vegan
- ◉ vegetarian
- ◉ whole food plant based
- ○ whole grain

NUTRITIONAL DATA:

calories	86.26
fat	2.54g
sat fat	0.29g
cholesterol	0mg
sodium	114.90mg
carbohydrates	12.61g
fiber	3.48g
sugars	2.09g
protein	4.05g

REFERENCES

1. "Putting the Brakes on Diabetes Complications," Centers for Disease Control and Prevention, last modified December 21, 2017, accessed January 4, 2018, https://www.cdc.gov/features/preventing-diabetes-complications/index.html.

2. "What Can I Drink?" American Diabetes Association web page, last modified September 20, 2017, accessed November 28, 2017, http://www.diabetes.org/food-and-fitness/food/what-can-i-eat/making-healthy-food-choices/what-can-i-drink.html.

3. Press release: "The American Diabetes Association Commends the Release of the 2015–2020 Dietary Guidelines for Americans to Promote Healthier Living," January 8, 2016, accessed November 28, 2017, http://www.diabetes.org/newsroom/press-releases/2016/2015-202-dietary-guidelines-to-promote-healthier-living.html.

4. "Diabetes Management Guidelines," National Diabetes Education Initiative web page, October 2013, accessed November 28, 2017, http://www.ndei.org/ADA-nutrition-guidelines-2013.aspx.html.

5. Alison B. Evert et al., "Nutrition Therapy Recommendations for the Management of Adults with Diabetes," Position Statement by the American Diabetes Association, Diabetes Care 36, no. 11 (November 2013): 3821–3842, https://doi.org/10.2337/dc13-2042.

6. "Protein Foods," American Diabetes Association web page, last modified October 16, 2017, accessed November 28, 2017, http://www.diabetes.org/food-and-fitness/food/what-can-i-eat/making-healthy-food-choices/meat-and-plant-based-protein.html.

7. "Fats," American Diabetes Association web page, last modified August 13, 2015, accessed November 28, 2017, http://www.diabetes.org/food-and-fitness/food/what-can-i-eat/making-healthy-food-choices/fats-and-diabetes.html.

8. "Diabetes Superfoods," American Diabetes Association web page, last modified October 11, 2017, accessed November 28, 2017, http://www.diabetes.org/food-and-fitness/food/what-can-i-eat/making-healthy-food-choices/diabetes-superfoods.html.

9. "Added Sugars," American Heart Association website, last modified February 1, 2017, accessed November 28, 2017, http://www.heart.org/HEARTORG/HealthyLiving/HealthyEating/Nutrition/Added-Sugars_UCM_305858_Article.jsp#.Wrpo32inGkw.

Acknowledgments

There are many people who have cared about this project as much as we have and we want to say thank you. Stephanie and Todd, thank you for inviting us to be part of such an exciting project. Susan and Lillian, we appreciate that you kept us on track and on schedule.   And to Chef James and Wendy, thank you for lending a helping hand.

Sherri:

I am grateful to my family that has always supported me no matter which road I've chosen to travel. Don and Fran, your support and encouragement are very much appreciated. And Edwin, thank you for all the laughter!

Edwin:

I would like to thank Anne Nechkov for showcasing the recipes with the understanding of creating each composition with the intention to promote health and create awareness of all the foods that are right at our fingertips. There are many people that made this project possible including Sherri Flynt, whose unconditional support and collaboration were essential for the balance created regarding the nutrition composition of the recipes. Thanks to Spencer and Kathy for their time, patience and awesome collaboration with the pictures. And to Don and Fran for supporting me during my years of professional growth within Nutritional Services. Lastly, thank you to my family and friends for supporting my career and believing that food is the path to wellness.

Edwin Cabrera
EXECUTIVE CHEF

Chef Edwin hails from the beautiful island of Puerto Rico. He made the decision to enter the culinary field after dancing classical ballet for fifteen years. After graduating from Scottsdale Culinary Institute in Arizona, he received his AA degree in Occupational Studies in Culinary Arts and Sciences, and Restaurant Management. He completed with honors the Nutrition, Diet, and Health Sciences course through Ashworth University.

Edwin currently serves as the Executive Chef at the Center for Nutritional Excellence with the AdventHealth Diabetes Institute. Since joining the Center, he has been focused on developing innovative recipes that reflect the principles of CREATION Health.

One of Edwin's greatest passions is working with the Center for Nutritional Excellence's dietitians and promoting healthy eating to residents of Central Florida.

Sherri Flynt, MPH, RD, LDN
REGISTERED DIETITIAN

Sherri Flynt serves as the Center for Nutritional Excellence Manager with the AdventHealth Diabetes Institute. She helped to establish the Center for Nutritional Excellence in 2001. As manager of the Center, Sherri works with a team of nutritional professionals dedicated to promoting healthier eating habits. The Center provides nutritional counseling and presentations, as well as assists AdventHealth Orlando service lines to enhance their programs by adding a nutrition touch.

Sherri holds a master's degree in public health as well as registered dietitian credentials from Loma Linda University. During her professional career, Sherri has presented hundreds of seminars, participated in numerous health fairs, and worked with countless executives, athletes, children, and families to achieve optimum health.
When Sherri isn't helping people make healthier lifestyle choices, she enjoys reading, gardening, going to the beach, and cheering for the Seattle Seahawks.

Erica Hechler, MS, RD, CDE
**REGISTERED DIETITIAN,
CERTIFIED DIABETES EDUCATOR**

Erica Hechler is an Orlando area based Registered Dietitian/Nutritionist, Certified Diabetes Educator and Health Coach. She has been in practice for over 20 years and specializes in diabetes and weight management. Her personal mission is to provide people with up-to-date, evidence-based nutrition and wellness information to help guide them through their nutrition and wellness vision. She hopes to inspire and empower clients to live well and to make choices that lead to positive lifelong habits and relationships with food.

She resides in Oviedo, Florida with her two daughters Jordan and Erinn. In her free time, she enjoys trying out new restaurants, listening to live music, meditating and enjoying the practice of yoga.

About AdventHealth Diabetes Institute

The AdventHealth Diabetes Institute is a national leader in diabetes care, patient education and research. Our multidisciplinary team of board-certified endocrinologists and providers specialize in a wide variety of services including management of prediabetes, gestational diabetes, type 1 and type 2 diabetes. We also provide comprehensive pre-diabetes and diabetes self-management education programs as well as weight management, RESET diabetes, and Thrive diabetes care programs that all focus on nutrition, exercise and medication management.

Whether you've recently been diagnosed with diabetes or want to focus on a particular aspect of diabetes management, we're here for you. Our certified diabetes educators are here to help you better understand ways to control your diabetes with a full spectrum of programs and ongoing support. We're honored that the AdventHealth Diabetes Institute Education Program has been recognized by the American Diabetes Association for Quality Self-Management Education* and Support. Our whole-person approach to healthcare empowers patients to develop and sustain lifestyle changes.

AdventHealth Diabetes Institute
2415 North Orange Avenue
Suite 501
Orlando, Florida 32804
(407) 303-2822

To learn more, visit
AdventHealthDiabetesInstitute.com

*The American Diabetes Association Recognizes this education service as meeting the National Standards for Diabetes Self-Management Education and Support.

DIABETES & ENDOCRINOLOGY

Among the Top 10% in the Country
AdventHealth is recognized by U.S. News & World Report as one of America's High Performing Hospitals for diabetes and endocrinology.

ABOUT THE PUBLISHER

AdventHealth is a connected network of care that promotes hope and healing through individualized care that touches the body, mind and spirit to help you feel whole. Our hospitals and care sites across the country are united by one mission: Extending the Healing Ministry of Christ. This faith-based mission guides our skilled and compassionate caregivers to provide expert care that leads the nation in quality, safety, and patient satisfaction.

Over 5 million people visit **AdventHealth** each year at our award-winning hospitals, physician practices, outpatient clinics, skilled nursing facilities, home health agencies and hospice centers to experience wholistic care for any stage of life and health.

AdventHealth Press publishes content rooted in wholistic health principles to help you feel whole through a variety of physical, emotional, and spiritual wellness resources. To learn more visit **AdventHealthPress.com**.

RECOGNITIONS

CLINICAL EXCELLENCE. AdventHealth hospital campuses have been recognized in the top five percent of hospitals in the nation for clinical excellence by Healthgrades. We believe that spiritual and emotional care, along with high-quality clinical care, combine to create the best outcome for our patients.

TOP SAFETY RATINGS. We care for you like we would care for our own loved ones – with compassion and a priority of safety. **AdventHealth's** hospitals have received grade "A" safety ratings from The Leapfrog Group, the only national rating agency that evaluates how well hospitals protect patients from medical errors, infections, accidents, and injuries.

SPECIALIZED CARE. For over ten years, **AdventHealth** hospitals have been recognized by U.S. News & World Report as "One of America's Best Hospitals" for clinical specialties such as: Cardiology and Heart Surgery, Orthopedics, Neurology and Neuroscience, Urology, Gynecology, Gastroenterology and GI Surgery, Diabetes and Endocrinology, Pulmonology, Nephrology, and Geriatrics.

AWARD-WINNING TEAM CULTURE. Becker's Hospital Review has recognized **AdventHealth** as a Top Place to Work in Healthcare based on diversity, team engagement and professional growth. **AdventHealth** has also been awarded for fostering an engaged workforce, meaning our teams are equipped and empowered in their work as they provide skilled and compassionate care.

WIRED FOR THE FUTURE. The American Hospital Association recognized **AdventHealth** as a "Most Wired" health system for using the latest technology and innovations to provide cutting-edge, connected care.

PARTNERSHIPS

SPORT LEAGUES. AdventHealth is the official hospital for the NBA's Orlando Magic, NFL's Tampa Bay Buccaneers, NHL's Tampa Bay Lightning, the Orlando Solar Bears, The University of Central Florida Knights, RunDisney, and sponsor of Daytona Speedweeks (NASCAR). In addition, AdventHealth has served as the exclusive medical care provider to many sports organizations such as Disney's Wide World of Sports, Walt Disney World's Marathon Weekend, the Capital One Bowl, and University of Central Florida Athletics. AdventHealth has also provided comprehensive healthcare services for the World Cup and the Olympics.

WALT DISNEY WORLD. AdventHealth has teamed up with the Walt Disney World® Resort to serve as the health and wellness resource partner that cares for cast members and guests from around the world. Disney and AdventHealth partnered to create a state-of-the-art children's hospital and a cutting-edge comprehensive health facility that was named the "Hospital of the Future" by the Wall Street Journal.

Index

Index

Index

Index

Index

Index

V

W

Y

Z

LEAD YOUR COMMUNITY
TO HEALTHY
LIVING

INCLUDES ONLINE TRAINING

Seminar Leader Kit

Everything a leader needs to conduct this seminar successfully, including key questions to facilitate group discussion and PowerPoint™ presentations for each of the eight principles.

Participant Guide

A study guide with essential information from each of the eight lessons along with outlines, self assessments, and questions for people to fill in as they follow along.

Small Group Kit

It's easy to lead a small group using the CREATION Health videos, the Small Group Leaders Guide, and the Small Group Discussion Guide.

CREATION Kids

CREATION Health Kids can make a big difference in homes, schools, and congregations. Lead kids in your community to healthier, happier living.

Life Guide Series

These guides include questions designed to help individuals or small groups study the depths of every principle and learn strategies for integrating them into everyday life.

ADDITIONAL RESOURCES

CREATION Health Discovery
Written by Des Cummings Jr., PhD, Monica Reed, MD, and Todd Chobotar, this wonderful companion resource introduces people to the CREATION Health philosophy and lifestyle.

CREATION Health Devotional
(English: Hardcover/Spanish: Softcover)
In this devotional you will discover stories about experiencing God's grace in the tough times, God's delight in triumphant times, and God's presence in peaceful times.

CREATION Health Devotional for Women
Written for women by women, the CREATION Health Devotional for Women is based on the principles of whole-person wellness represented in CREATION Health. Spirits will be lifted and lives rejuvenated by the message of each unique chapter.

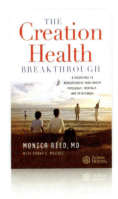

CREATION Health Breakthrough
Blending science and lifestyle recommendations, Monica Reed, MD, prescribes eight essentials that will help reverse harmful health habits and prevent disease. Discover how intentional choices, rest, environment, activity, trust, relationships, outlook, and nutrition can put a person on the road to wellness.

CREATION Health One-Sentence Journal
The CREATION Health One-Sentence Journal is a simple, fun, and powerful tool to transform your life. It takes just moments a day. Yet the effect it can have over time is life-changing.

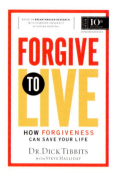

Forgive To Live (English: Hardcover / Spanish: Softcover)

In *Forgive to Live: How Forgiveness Can Save Your Life,* Dr. Tibbits presents the scientifically proven steps for forgiveness—taken from the first clinical study of its kind conducted by Stanford University and Florida Hospital.

The Love Fight

Are you going to fight for love or against each other? The authors illustrate how this common encounter can create a mutually satisfying relationship. Their expertise will walk you through the scrimmage between those who want to accomplish and those who want to relate.

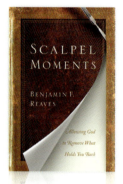

Scalpel Moments

A scalpel moment can be one of painful awareness, disturbing clarity, sorrowful regret. It can also be a moment of positive awakening that can reveal, restore, and renew. Ordained minister Dr. Reaves highlights stories about life's difficult or revealing moments that remove layers of confusion, bitterness, or fear and restore one's trust in God.

SuperSized Kids

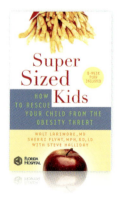

In *SuperSized Kids: How to Rescue Your Child from The Obesity Threat,* Walt Larimore, MD, and Sherri Flynt, MPH, RD, LD, explains step by step, how parents can work to avert the coming childhood obesity crisis by taking control of the weight challenges facing every member of their family.

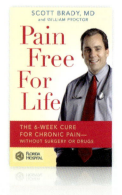

Pain Free For Life

In *Pain Free For Life,* Scott C. Brady, MD,—founder of Florida Hospital's Brady Institute for Health—leads pain-racked readers to a pain-free life using powerful mind-body-spirit strategies —where more than 80 percent of his chronic-pain patients achieved 80–100 percent pain relief within weeks.

Organizations

**American Association
of Diabetes Educators**

200 W. Madison St
Suite 800
Chicago, IL 60606
800-338-3633
www.diabeteseducator.org

**American Diabetes Association
Attn: National Call Center**

2451 Crystal Drive, Suite 900
Arlington, VA 22202
800-342-2383 (800-DIABETES)
www.diabetes.org

Diabetes Canada - National Office

1400-522 University Ave.
Toronto, O N M5G 2R5, Canada
800-226-8464
www.diabetes.ca

**Centers for Disease Control and
Prevention, Division of Diabetes
Translation**

1600 Clifton Road
Atlanta, GA 303-29-4027
800-232-4636
www.cdc.gov/diabetes

**Diabetes Exercise and
Sports Association**

8001 Montcastle Drive
Nashville,TN 37221
800-898-4322
www.diabetes-exercise.org

International Diabetes Federation

166 Chaussee de La Hulpe
B-1170 Brussels, Belgium
+32-2-53855 I I
www.idf.org

**Juvenile Diabetes Research
Foundation International**

26 Broadway, 14th Floor
New York, NY 10004
800-533-2873 (800-533-CURE)
www.jdrf.org

**National Diabetes
Education Program**

9000 Rockville Pike
Bethesda, MD 20892
800-860-8747
www.ndep.nih.gov

**National Diabetes
Information Clearinghouse**

9000 Rockville Pike
Bethesda, MD 20892
800-860-8747
www.diabetes.niddk.nih.gov

**National Kidney Disease
Education Program**

9000 Rockville Pike
Bethesda, MD 20892
800-8860-8747
www.nkdep.nih.gov

National Kidney Foundation

30 E, 33rd St.
New York, NY 10016
800-622-9010
www.kidney.org

**United Network for Organ Sharing
(UNOS)**

700 N. 4th Street
Richmond, VA 23219
804-782-4800
www.unos.org

We Would Like To Hear From You

Visit our website and
send us your comment
about this cookbook.

ADVENTHEALTHPRESS.COM